Towards Identity in the Psychoanalytic Encounter

Towards Identity in the Psychoanalytic Encounter addresses the theme of identification and identity in the psychoanalytic clinic as elaborated by Jacques Lacan over the course of his teaching.

In psychoanalysis, the subject who is summoned "to speak himself" is by definition lacking in identity. His question is "What am I?" but, as he is only represented by his words, his being is "always elsewhere", within other words that are yet to come. Thus a paradox: one seeks via speech the identity of a being who, through his speech, is not identifiable. Yet the fact remains, he has a body, and he is riveted to sufferings that psychoanalysis, from Freud to Lacan, identified, which are not accidental, which we call repetition and symptom, and which shift the question of identity because a One, real, is at play in them.

Towards Identity in the Psychoanalytic Encounter will be key reading for the study and research of Lacanian psychoanalysis and all practitioners interested in Lacan's teaching, as well as other discourses such as philosophy, art, literature and history.

Colette Soler practices and teaches psychoanalysis in Paris. She holds an agrégation in philosophy and a doctorate in psychology. It was her encounter with the teaching and person of Jacques Lacan that led her to choose psychoanalysis. She was a member of the École Freudienne de Paris and, following its dissolution, became the Director of the École de la Cause Freudienne, after which she was at the forefront of the movement of the International of the Forums and its School of Psychoanalysis.

Towards Identity in the Psychoanalytic Encounter

A Lacanian Perspective

Colette Soler

Translated by

Chantal Degril, Camille Germanos,
David Kirkman, Devra Simiu and Daphne Tamarin

Routledge
Taylor & Francis Group

LONDON AND NEW YORK

First published in English 2024
by Routledge
4 Park Square, Milton Park, Abingdon, Oxon OX14 4RN

and by Routledge
605 Third Avenue, New York, NY 10158

Routledge is an imprint of the Taylor & Francis Group, an informa business

© 2024 Colette Soler

Translated by Chantal Degril, Camille Germanos, David Kirkman, Devra Simiu and Daphne Tamarin

The right of Colette Soler to be identified as author of this work has been asserted in accordance with sections 77 and 78 of the Copyright, Designs and Patents Act 1988.

Published in French by Éditions du Champ lacanien 2015 as Vers l'identité

British Library Cataloguing-in-Publication Data
A catalogue record for this book is available from the British Library

ISBN: 978-1-032-64549-0 (hbk)
ISBN: 978-0-367-34203-6 (pbk)
ISBN: 978-1-032-64550-6 (ebk)

DOI: 10.4324/9781032645506

Typeset in Times New Roman
by Apex CoVantage, LLC

In loving memory of Doctor Nestor Tamarin, member of the International School of Psychoanalysis of the Lacanian Field, founding member of the Forums of Israel and London, psychiatrist, psychoanalyst, enthusiastic and generous teacher of psychoanalysis and our very dear friend, without whom this work would not have been possible.

Contents

Preface

Towards Identity is the second in an ongoing series of translations into English of the annual seminar given by Colette Soler at the Clinical College of the School of Psychoanalysis of the Forums of the Lacanian Field in Paris.

Hands down, today's leading commentator on the works of Jacques Lacan, Colette Soler, in her annual seminars, not only teaches and transmits Lacanian theory but also challenges and pushes it, forging new and vital pathways for thinking psychoanalysis into the future.

The idea to translate Soler's annual seminars into English originated with Daphne and Nestor Tamarin, who recognized the crucial role of the seminars and the importance of making them available to the English-speaking community and beyond.

This translation of Soler's 2014–2015 seminar, *Vers l'identité*, is the work of a Cartel on Translation, five who came together (via Zoom) from various English-speaking forums of the School, each one animated by a singular desire, a singular question, and guided by the Cartel's plus-one, Nestor Tamarin who, sadly, during the course of the Cartel's work passed away and to whom this translation is dedicated.

Translation of any kind is rooted in optimism, the belief that one can capture and transmit something from one mind to another, one language to another. Sustained by this optimism, week after week for almost three years, the members of the Cartel met to engage with the text and to . . . make it speak English!

Never one to mince words, always razor-sharp in her delivery and precise in her choice of words, Colette Soler presents her annual seminars to a live audience in Paris at the School of the IF-EPFCL. The goals of the Cartel on Translation were thus twofold: clarity for the English-speaking reader; and fidelity to Soler's style, including the precision of her word choices and her specific reading of difficult-to-transmit Lacanian concepts. With these two goals in mind, the Cartel often found itself rather joyfully spending hours discussing a single page or paragraph, a single phrase or word. In a nod to the problematics of any translation, the Cartel, at various points, made the decision to provide the French phrase or word alongside the English.

The importance of Soler's text, *Towards Identity*, goes far beyond anything that can be described here. Beginning from a rather small question – why the concept of identity figures far less often in psychoanalytic texts than that of identification – Soler takes up the task of first uncovering, then meticulously elucidating what could be called a quite significant misunderstanding about the place of identity in Lacanian psychoanalysis. Daring to attribute this misunderstanding to some of Lacan's own teachings, Soler carefully demonstrates that identity at the end of analysis was always the "target" for Lacan, always his saying, in spite of the fact that he formulated and reformulated it in many different ways. Identity at the end of analysis, but not just any kind. As Soler says, this identity does not pass through identification; it "does not borrow from the Other of discourse". She calls it "an identity of separation".

The relevance of *Towards Identity* extends as well to what is happening today in our larger world. Clinician and non-clinician alike will find in this text an invaluable tool for assessing and contributing to pivotal, contemporary debates on the topic of identity.

Chapter 1

12th November 2014

The two terms of our title for this year, *identity* and *identification,* do not have the same presence in the psychoanalytic literature although they are well represented and even familiar in common discourse. This already gives us a clue that analytic discourse tackles the issue in a specific way.

Analytic context

The term *identification* was introduced by Freud at the very beginning. It is insistent, and it has even been convoked within the IPA, to define the change at the end of analysis with the notion of identification with the analyst, which outraged Lacan so much. The term has not only been used in psychoanalysis from the outset, but it is proliferating. How many different types of identification can be picked out? All the so-called oedipal identifications, with dad, with mum and a few others around, siblings in particular, and then the identifications of the boy with his band of mates and of the girl with her friend. And on a more theoretical level, Freud's three identifications in *Group Psychology and the Analysis of the Ego* when he tries to specify some types, reread by Lacan, as well as the two identifications constitutive of the crowds, the identifications of the ego, the identifications by means of the symptom. Furthermore, in Lacan's work, the identification with the image in the mirror, the identification with I(A), the identification with the almighty signifier of the demand, the identification with desire, the immediate identifications in psychosis that suppose others, themselves mediated, the identification with the phallus, the identification with the object, and I am certainly forgetting some. Therefore, it will not be fruitless, as we move along, to define what identifications are and the function they fulfil but most of all to grasp what is the logic of this proliferation.

On the other hand, in contrast, the term *identity* is almost not there. And it is noticeable that very often analysts do not receive it favourably, and they occasionally put forward the absence of the term in order to conclude that it is not an analytic issue or even claim that analysis leads up to, and should lead up to, non-identity. We can ask ourselves: Why this reserve? Could this be because, in society, identity is first and foremost a matter of social control and thus of police that indeed only have one phrase: "Your papers?" Papers that ensure your civic identity or otherwise, it

DOI: 10.4324/9781032645506-1

is well known, the "undocumented" ["*sans papiers*"] is a suspect by definition. But in fact, is it not clear that every discourse, insofar as it establishes a social link, that is to say, an order, produces a comparable operation? I mean that they require from us something that is equivalent to identity papers. At university, diplomas secure your identity as a graduate. Even in psychoanalysis – although everything proceeds through speech, without written certification, and moreover where one is not compelled to attend – when speaking of an entry threshold, is it not to say that an identity, let's say, an analysand's identity, is required? And then there is the hysteric's request: "Let me see if you are a man". As a matter of fact, since each discourse requires showing one's credentials, is it not the same thing?

Thus, why this reserve among analysts? And I am talking here about the Lacanian current. Not finding the word *identity*, could it be that they conclude that the thing is absent, that the question of identity is absent? Obviously, the word and the thing is a contested expression – an entire literature is linked to it – because one might say, as Lacan does, that the word makes the thing or that there is no fact but from being said, as he also puts it. I am not going to enter into such a vast debate, thus, I am amending it: we must distinguish the word from the theme it refers to. Admittedly, *identification* is the word in vogue in psychoanalysis, but what is the function or the aim of an identification, whatever it may be, if it is not to ensure some identity? Here too, I may add, some identity, whatever it may be. As a result, one has to understand that under the problem of identifications lies the theme of identity that runs across the entire teaching of Lacan from beginning to end.

Identity convokes at the same time difference and identicality. It is almost the same word. Your own identity sets you apart from everyone else, from any other, but this trait of difference implies that you remain identical to yourself, notwithstanding potential transformations. When Lacan says that analysis aims at an absolute difference – and we all know the resounding success of this saying among us – what is it, other than a form of radical identity in its difference and its stability? When he speaks about the function of the letter of the symptom, to be distinguished from the signifier because it is the only one that is identical to itself (Lacan, 1975), thus outside of dialectic, is he not aiming at determining what can ensure identity?

Whenever one seeks to ensure identity, these two identity traits – the one of difference and the one of identicality – are convoked throughout the entire social discourse, and, for instance, they determine specific social practices for purposes of detecting characteristic features both distinctive and forgery-proof, what used to be called "distinguishing marks" on identity cards. Fingerprints that are forgery-proof, although they can be removed; voice modulation frequency, so it seems; DNA, said to be truly unfalsifiable; all of the above are not traits of particularity but of singularity, namely peculiar to one and one only. On the same level, it could be amusing to enquire about all the falsification practices that have been developed with so much ingenuity throughout history in order to cover an identity, in the domain of espionage, for instance, or in order to escape from police investigations. Obviously, the identity traits that are focused on in these practices are bodily characteristics and not characteristics of the subject per se. I am only mentioning them at this point for the sake of emphasising that the guaranteed identification of an individual, to be distinguished from a subject, falls back on discriminating traits. Clearly, when I mention the endeavours to identify identities, the question only has meaning within a social link where it is, let us say, the social Other that seeks to identify individuals with specific procedures that are scientific nowadays, whereas individuals can themselves have some reasons to hide their own identity and to protect it – now called "personal data protection". The question arises differently in psychoanalysis, but in summary one cannot identify an identity, that is to say, grasp the uniqueness of its difference without what we can call a One, a forgery-proof One. Now, what about the subjects of psychoanalysis?

Consciousness of identity

Psychoanalysis deals with the subjects who speak, and what it cannot but encounter is, first of all, the phenomenon of self-consciousness [*conscience de soi*] that includes the proper name and memory, with the various stages of life regardless of the changes they bring. Therefore, this self-consciousness inevitably depends on a sense of identity that does not require additional foundation and is not put into question. Sometimes we even see subjects strongly perceiving, in certain circumstances, the impossibility inherent in everyone to break loose from themselves, or even the uncanniness of being oneself, riveted to a body that locates you in space – this is probably why we can dream of invisibility and ubiquity – and to a memory which situates you in time. Certainly, much has been achieved by Lacan in order to establish that these temporal and spatial coordinates that determine self-consciousness are subordinated to language and therefore are not simple natural phenomena, but this does not take anything away from their existential evidence. As a result, how can the identity proper to each one become a question? How can the sense of identity be called into question, and not only in psychoanalysis?

Outside the field of psychoanalysis, there is an extreme phenomenon, probably the most extreme, namely, identity amnesia, the joint loss of the proper name and of the personalised past linked to it. Lacan mentions it because it shows that human memory is not simply the insertion of the living [*du vivant*] in reality, but that it implies – I quote – "the subject's link to a discourse where he can be suppressed [*réprimé*], that is to say not know that this discourse implicates him" (Lacan, [1970] 2001, p. 334). The proof is precisely by identity amnesia, that remarkably does not cause the loss of "benefit of the learned" [*aucun bénéfice de l'appris*] but suspends the sense of identity, the name and self-consciousness, which are, for that matter, recoverable without organic treatment.

To put the sense of identity into question, there are also less extreme, even banal, phenomena. It could be summed up in the amusing expression: "I am not what you think I am". In other words, all the experiences where the subject confronts, with noisy or silent protest, the identity verdicts of the Other – all of its "you are" . . . this or that. These phenomena are particularly acute in adolescence for fundamental reasons. I am calling verdicts of the Other all the judgments of attribution that it applies to the subject and whose signifiers, Lacan said, "are an affront" to the subject who sees itself as other than the words that are plastered on its reality, but without being able to say what other it is – hence the yearning to "have one's voice heard" which is believed to solve the problem. And so, the assertion coming from the Other, be it familial or social, can spontaneously raise for a subject the question of its true identity. This phenomenon electively occurs in adolescence, although not exclusively, and we understand why. It is because adolescence is a time when the professional, familial or even sexual status that strengthens the social identity of each one is pending. Sometimes, that is all it takes to motivate a demand to the analyst who we know, if he is an analyst, by definition aims beyond the verdicts and the norms of the Other.

If what psychoanalysis has called the ego is the set of images – the image of the body included – and of signifiers that identify the social or socialised individual, therefore, we are able to conceive that what Lacan calls subject is the part of the being that is not identified – not identified by these images and these signifiers. In saying *signifier*, I am certainly taking a shortcut, but is there anything in the social being, whether it be a matter of their sex, family, school or profession, etc., that does not pass through signifiers? What is it, then, of the subject that is not identified and that still remains as the unity of all the identifying traits? Is it not what in other places is called the soul? I was listening on the radio to François Cheng, who was interviewed every day for one week at the end of last October, and he was evoking the soul and the encounter of souls as the encounter with what makes each one unique, ineffably unique, of course. In psychoanalysis, we do not speak of the soul but of the subject.

Identity called into question

The construction of the structure of the subject by Lacan is certainly complex; it took him years, but what it comes down to is as simple as what I have just said and is not only at stake in analytic discourse – besides, the term subject does not come from religion but from philosophy.

What is proper to psychoanalysis is that it begins with the calling into question of identity consciousness and with the so-called question of the subject. I have already indicated that this question is present in common discourse but, beyond being widely misrecognised, how is it dealt with? We can say that each one is invited to coincide as much as possible with his or her own social identity. It is also strongly suggested to him that he is responsible for it because we are living in the era of resilience and of the *self-made man*. Two notions of success that enjoin us to underestimate, on the one hand, the contingencies and the accidents of history and, on the other hand, the destiny created for us by inheritance. Psychoanalysis does the opposite. At the moment of entry, it encourages the one who consults to call into question his/her feeling of identity if this has not already happened by chance of circumstances. We often repeat that we are seeing those who suffer. We need to put an end to this stupidity. Certainly, we are seeing those who suffer, but incidentally, who does not suffer? Distress does not suffice for entering into analytic discourse. As we say and as Freud said, althoughin other terms, if there is a threshold to be crossed, it is because the one who suffers speaks as a subject of consciousness who knows his own difficulties and distress and asks you to work things out. How to transform a sufferer who knows how to suffer into a subject who does not know, a subject supposed by what causes his distress, supposed as an unknown, in the mathematical sense of the term? Lacan has even evoked the unknown of an equation, x, for which the solution will have to be found. We also speak about a question that awaits an answer. How can we substitute the one who shows up – who is not a supposed one and who is right here in front of you – with the subject lacking identity and so possibly seeking some?

The history of psychoanalysis gives a good example: Dora. Nowadays, we would say a teen – as she is eighteen at a time when reaching the age of majority was much later – that is causing problems within the family. This is the case. So she is brought before Freud, and she begins by pleading her cause, her indignation in the face of her father's liaison with Frau K. It is the discourse of righteous outrage. Probably a nice description of the hidden sides of an upper-middle-class family but not a single subject supposed, and the family runs no risk of undergoing an analysis. Then Freud manages to show her that she has not always been complaining about it and that she has also been an active accomplice for a long time and absolutely delighted about the whole affair. She does not deny it; she acknowledges it without being able to explain it. Here we have a little enigma, or at least a question, and this strange complicity becomes the signifier of the subject exposed to the contradictions in its behaviour. We know what comes next. Freud, after that brilliant start – and being called to answer: "What do you think about it, Professor?" – provokes the cessation of the treatment himself. This is what I call a "true interruption", and this is what is most demonstrative in the case: the treatment ends because as soon as the question arose, Freud tried to put an end to it by giving the answer while he furthermore congratulates himself for bringing to her notice that she loves Herr K. Dora's answer is prompt: nothing much was revealed, she said and left. The problem is not whether the interpretation is right or wrong but the fact that it saturated the question of the subject. Incidentally, we know how much Freud was preoccupied for many years with that failure. He went back over it very often and, certainly, his own position with respect to feminine mystery played a part in it, he who wanted – Lacan has noted – his fiancée to tell him . . . everything. Anyway, let's move on.

In the same fashion, a symptom recognised as such, but especially a dream, precisely because it is an enigma by definition, may constitute an entry point into analysis. One might as well say that at the entry, transference is put in place only when the supposition of an unidentified subject arises. It is what we have to bring about in the patient, against common discourse and especially against the discourse of care, the *care* that masks it.

The trajectory of a psychoanalytic treatment can therefore be clearly outlined: at the beginning, the question, at the end, the answer to be produced; at the beginning, the unidentified subject and at the end, one can expect the identity of the subject. We could think that Lacan's teaching follows a homologous trajectory: at the beginning, the theory of the subject as unknown, supposed to the Freudian unconscious, and at the end, the emphasis on the identity of jouissance. Indeed, even before "The Function and Field of Speech and Language", the identity in question was there, with his first original contribution to psychoanalysis "The Mirror Stage" in 1936. The original text has been lost, but the 1949 version remains. Before, we have his thesis on Aimée, but it does not deal with psychoanalysis, and also "Les complexes familiaux", a very interesting text which remains within the frame of classic Freudian psychoanalysis. He himself has not included the latter in his "On My Antecedents", and it is no accident. His "Mirror Stage" describes a first identification with the image of oneself in the mirror. What is it supposed to accomplish if not to ensure a first identity by means of the form of the body and moreover an identity that is offered to the appreciation of the one who is looking at it? Lacan has critiqued this imaginary identity of the ego by underlining its alienating character, a principle of misrecognition – misrecognition of the unknown that is the subject that speaks. Besides, it is certain that in the end, he insists on what makes identity, whether it is the object or the symptom. However, the homology between the trajectory of analysis and the trajectory of Lacan's elaborations is only an apparent one because he has marked since the beginning, and step by step, the necessity of an end of analysis by means of identity.

At the different stages of his teaching, the target of identity constitutes what I call an invariant, in various formulas. But it is not any identity. It is what I call an "identity of separation" (Soler, 2004, p. 114). This expression is not in Lacan, but it conveys his thesis, which is precisely that of an identity that does not pass through an identification that draws a few traits from the Other. Let us have a look at it step by step.

Towards identity

I shall begin at the end with the formula that came as such a surprise: the ending by means of "identification with the symptom". It was the ironic tit-for-tat answer to the IPA that talked about the identification with the analyst. Nowadays, this notion seems incredible, and the so-called identification with the analyst, when one thinks one can diagnose it, is always considered a sign of failure. The expression "identification with the symptom" may come as a surprise and may even appear paradoxical because the symptom is the common name of what analysis is supposed to treat. Let me note, moreover, that most analysts of the EFP, if they did not reject it outright, saw in it a great novelty. What is certain is that the years ranging from 1970 to 1975 are characterised by change in Lacan's work: the new schema of the Borromean knot and, together with it, new clinical breakthroughs, the depreciation of the hegemony of the symbolic, the reassessment of the real, the redefinition of the symptom that is no longer considered as a problem but as a solution to the non-relationship, etc. However, up to what point does this reversal of perspectives change what has to be achieved at the end of analysis? I emphasised that the formulas of Lacan may change, but his saying does not. From beginning to end, it all comes down to reaching an identity that does not borrow from the Other of discourse, as do all the other identities passing through an identification that I call "identities of alienation".

This saying about the end through identity of separation is generalisable. There is no other saying of Lacan regarding the term and the result of analytic metamorphosis. It ranges from the ineffable identity stated from 1949 up to the identity that the jouissance letter of the symptom snatches from the ineffable – the letter being the only thing in language identical to itself – passing through full speech that enables the subject to become "identical to himself" (Lacan, [1955] 2006, p. 291), and then subjective destitution. I will return to the demonstration later, but I already pointed out that, from beginning to end, what is under construction in Lacan's teaching is the end by identity of separation.

Identity is the opposite of going astray; separation, the opposite of subjection. It is astonishing to realise up to what point Lacan produced misunderstanding and was misunderstood by his first students. They have successively elevated to pathos and, therefore, to an ideal: lack, castration, disbeing [*désêtre*], destitution, without forgetting non-knowledge and non-identity. Hence their stupefaction when identification with the symptom appeared, which, however, was only placing the ultimate quilting point on a thesis present from the beginning, although expressed in different terms – because in order to reach this last formulation, a redefinition of the function of the symptom was required beforehand. Lacan himself diagnosed this misunderstanding by evoking the analysts who "authorise themselves only by going astray" [*s'autorisent que de leur égarement*] (Lacan, [1975] 2001, p. 314).

In fact, Lacan, in spite of himself, is principally responsible for what I call here misunderstanding, in the true sense of the term. It is his definition of the subject which is the cause of this misunderstanding due to a lack of clarification. Lacan's major advance, while walking in Freud's footsteps, was to have grasped that the existence of the unconscious, as demonstrated in the Freudian practice, implied a subversion of the classic notion of the subject. A subversion that is lodged in the notion of a "divided subject" developed by Lacan over the course of nearly twenty years, contra the subject of psychological consciousness and contra the subject of philosophy, which itself is never thought of as a divided subject. Against the epistemic subject about which Emmanuel Kant said, "The *I think* must be able to accompany all my representations", against that of phenomenology, and I think even against that of the Cartesian cogito to which Lacan, nonetheless, refers the subject of psychoanalysis – all of this, of course, would require further explanations. It was against the pseudo-evidence of psychology and of philosophy that Lacan had to build the structure of the subject who speaks in analysis; an analysis where it turns out that the subject has an unconscious that thinks without him, there where this subject of self-consciousness that I evoked is not.

I would say that Lacan spent years responding to the emergency, that is to say, explaining that the one who says "I" is not a One, teaching that he has to learn that he is, I quote, "some two" and, far from being identical to himself, there is at least himself and his unconscious, the signifiers by which he represents himself, and those of his unconscious that he will decipher. It was a matter of urgency because of what psychoanalysis had become after the War since Anna Freud had brought cognitivism into it before its time, as I have already mentioned. She did it by bringing back to the fore the consideration of the ego and by postulating that this ego is equipped with a knowledge apparatus disjoined from libido, thus autonomous. It was precisely the hypothesis of cognitivism but before its time.

To the question: "Why this misunderstanding?" I, therefore, answer: Because he managed to convey his conception of the subverted subject of psychoanalysis, that is, a subject "without identity". Incidentally, this is how Serge Leclaire formulated it in 1979 during the last Congress of the EFP on the pass, and Lacan did not say no, except that it is only true regarding the subject insofar as it is supposed to language but not the subject that Lacan himself later qualified as real in *RSI*.

References

Lacan, J. (1975). *R.S.I. Seminaire XXII (1974–1975) leçon du 21 Janvier 1975* [Unpublished manuscript].

Lacan, J. (2001 [1970]). La méprise du sujet supposé savoir. In: *Autres écrits* (pp. 329–339). Paris: Éditions du Seuil.

Lacan, J. (2001 [1975]). Peut-être à Vincennes. In: *Autres écrits* (pp. 313–315). Paris: Éditions du Seuil.

Lacan, J. (2006 [1955]). Variations on the Standard Treatment. In: *Écrits: The First Complete Edition in English*. B. Fink (Trans.). New York: Norton.

Soler, C. (2004). Les invariants de l'analyse finie. *Hétérité*, 5, pp. 113–121.

Chapter 2

26th November 2014

Last time, I introduced the question of the year by way of its context in the analytic movement, the key element of this context being the theory of the subject of psychoanalysis, elaborated by Lacan, in fact, a non-identified subject, even non-identifiable. Hence, I suppose, the reservations on the part of Lacanians with regard to what one calls identity. I would now like to situate the question in its other context, that of the common discourse current in the capitalist regime. I believe it is necessary to pay attention to this context, for it has effects and an impact on the question that concerns us. For psychoanalysis, this impact is only partially determinate since, for it, what is fundamental to identity and identification is not capitalism but rather the status of what we call the subject. I will come back to this as it is what interests me, but first, I have to ask in what way and to what extent capitalism changes today's subjects. The question does not originate with me, it has already been posed, and diverse voices say that it renders them unanalysable.

"Apparolé" to capitalism[1]

Capitalism, which would not exist without science, has transformed what we call the world. It has radically modified it and continues to modify the means of production – this is what Marx took as his object of study. It has moreover upended the biological economy of the planet, what we call nature, but more importantly for us, it also modifies subjectivities from the inside. Subjectivities, by which we mean those who speak, conscious of themselves and their place in society, have always been historical. And today, it is clear that the discourse that develops in the capitalist economy infiltrates the individuals caught up in this economy. This is not to say that the subjects of capitalism are new subjects; subjects simply follow the evolution of the order in which they are placed as psychological and social subjects, and this is nothing new: psychological and social subjects have always been intimately tied to the discourse of their time. This is, incidentally, what one calls adaptation, subjectivities adjusting themselves to the requirements of the social link which orders all the bodily habits (food, social posturing, clothing, fashion, management of violence, and even of sex) but also the whole of thinking, with its prejudices and historical values. Freud said nothing else when, in "The Ego and the

DOI: 10.4324/9781032645506-2

Id", he claimed that the ego, which, for him, is not the whole of the individual, is formed by identification with familial and social authorities. Thus, we do not have new subjects; we have a new discourse to which subjects adapt from the inside and which, if I may say so, has always been the case. Lacan says nicely: the subject who speaks is a subject "apparolé" to the discourse in which he dwells. What does this mean? The order of discourse precedes them, and subjects speak the language and idiom of their time. This does not simply mean that they receive from it, let's say, the blah-blah, vocabulary, syntax and themes; it goes much further than this, for idiom and language have real effects: they preside over the adjustment not of the word, but of what is of the living [du vivant] or, to put it differently, over the modalities of jouissance ordered by each discourse. What Lacan constructed and named discourse knots the structure of language and its effects into what is not language, that is, the living. Nothing new in this regard.

At most, we can open the chapter on the subjective effects of today's capitalism on subjects "*apparolé*" to it. They are obvious. In the narratives that capitalism requires in order to function, it is not only that the human being is reduced to merchandise, to the object of exchange; one is now "human capital" or a "human resource". In 2004, a CEO of TF1 boasted about "selling available human brain time". All this is obvious, but there is more to it, namely that money as a value now holds the upper hand in the inner judgments of the majority of individuals. Consequently, and more now than ever, the poverty of the poor is redoubled by the shame of being poor. As for profitability, an economic value, it has become an individual value, a sort of personal superego that incites one to accomplish a great deal in a minimum of time. The subjectivities of our time have become managers of themselves. They say, for example, "I cannot succeed in managing this feeling, my relationship, my family, my body, my sexuality, etc.". It is as if each one were pushed to function like a kind of self-enterprise, with a plan of action to acquire competencies, make his "employability" flourish and manage his professional abilities. As a result, the psychological dispositions, emotional and relational – in short, the whole of character –are treated as commodities, with coaches of every kind monitoring their output. Let me add, given that time management and profitability are indissociable, time within schedules is adapted to the norms of the market and of competition (Baschet, 2014). Everyone complains about it, but no one escapes it.

Identity and the social link

Now, in this context of contemporary capitalism, identity has become a problem, a matter for polemics; and this is probably not unconnected to the fact that we, analysts, are posing this question for psychoanalysis. In fact, what prompted me to place emphasis on the effect of context at the beginning of this year was a suggestion made to me by an excellent colleague, who asked me to speak on the theme of "identity and segregation". This theme does not come from psychoanalysis, but from our time, that's for sure, although psychoanalysis can say something about it. It inserts itself within a larger question: What relation is there between the identities of individuals and the social link? As I said, in reality, in the social link, each one is already identified by the Other; in other words, they are always labelled under identity indexes. Listen to how various news items are reported on the radio. For example, "a 45-year-old woman, mother of three, unemployed"; "a 60-year-old homeless person, originally from . . . ". The discourse hands each one a sort of identity mirror from which he cannot exit and which is constituted from a constellation of signifiers, those of sex, age (thus the body), origin (thus native tongue), family (thus history), religion (thus choice), education, profession (thus competence), etc. These indexes come from discourse and determine what I am going to call social identity, that which is attributed. This social or discursive identity, I have called an identity of . . . alienation. The way it works today yields specific subjective phenomena.

First of all, we see that everyone aspires to an identity. This was not always the case, not only because modern individualism did not always exist, but also because traditional societies, less mobile, assigned places and prescribed roles based on birth; and because social control, certainly not less significant than it is today, albeit different, instead inspired individuals to vow to escape it. Thus one aspires to an identity, to make a name for oneself, to make a place for oneself. These phenomena have become acute because capitalism pushes individualism to an extreme and undoes social links. In this context, the individual, which I said is always already identified, is divided between opposite wishes. Indeed he aspires to an identity but not just any random identity: an identity that is valorised, valorisable, distinctive. There are, in fact, two contradictory wishes which gnaw at today's individuals. On the one hand, to be like everyone else, one aspires to integration by way of conformism – we know the complaint: "I don't succeed in being like others" – and, failing this, there is a sense of abnormality and the anguish of exclusion. On the other hand, one aspires to distinguish oneself, "the subject says no" to the attributed identity – "I am not what you think I am" – he claims a different identity, and when that fails, there is a feeling of being mundane, banal, invisible, etc. These are established facts.

You see how the question of identity is relevant for showing the subjective effects of common discourse. I had the idea that using Euler's Circles, which Lacan introduces in Seminar XI, we could represent the relationship between individuals as individuated organisms and the order of discourse wherein their own history is placed. I am submitting this to you, although it is only a first approximation, ultimately insufficient. In the intersection between a circle representing the Other and a circle representing what, in the text, he called "being", Lacan wrote what these two fields have or could have in common: the signifier and/or the lack. With these two circles, I write on one side the individuated organism; on the other, the discursive order as the treasury of the identity indexes, let us say, the unary traits of identity. The individual who is caught there thus becomes the subject of this identity of alienation about which I am speaking.

Obviously, this is not the whole of his identity, hence the insufficiency of the schema. This jumps out at you, for in this distribution, we can already ask where is the unconscious, the subject of the unconscious, that interests the psychoanalyst.

The unconscious is clearly not the secret; a secret is a concealed knowledge, subtracted from the Other; there is something of the secret in each individual, and it is

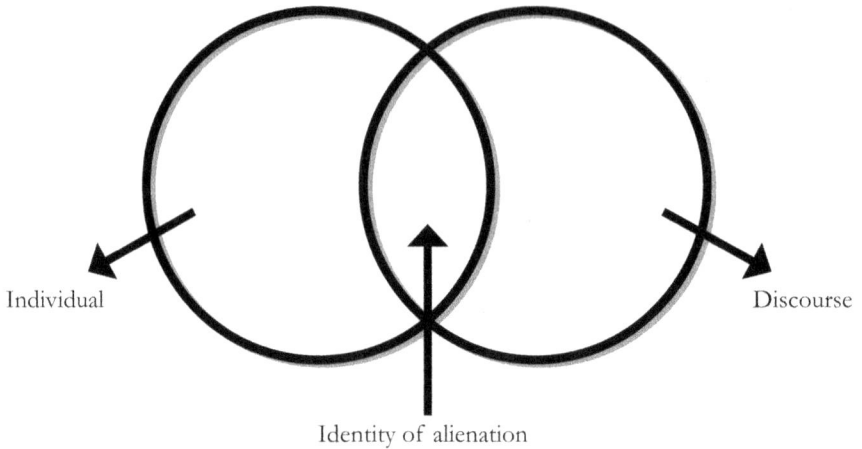

Individual   Discourse

Identity of alienation

Figure 2.1 The identity of alienation

certainly not only secret bank accounts. But what is subtracted from the exchange of speech, even the most intimate, has nothing to do with the unconscious which is articulated just as much as speech, yet nevertheless "unknown" [*insu*]; this is the right term. What one calls the private is therefore divided between what is dissimulated, the secret, those secrets that today we chase after in the name of transparency, and what is more radically unknown. But what is important is that this unknown is equally on the side of discourse, for on both sides, there is something of language and of the effect of language. This is a point to take up later. For the moment, I return to the logic of segregation.

The segregative option

It is the logic of segregation which makes up for the social link when it is in default. The role of the social link, as defined by Lacan, is to deal with differences by way of an order. This is why disparity, which today has such bad press, is inherent to the social link. I believe I developed this last year. All of the discursive couples, master/slave, professor/student, hysteric/master signifier and analyst/analysand are marked by disparity. What happens in a regime that tends to accomplish the parity of individuals? This is what capitalism does in the pathway marked by science. Universalism has been introduced by science, which, by definition, excludes from consideration what is singular. Dedicated to finding what constitutes law in each of its fields, it forecloses the singular subject. Capitalism realises this foreclosure and constitutes it as a reality in the world under the form of homogenisation since it knows nothing of beings except their function in the productive machine. Human rights duplicate this real homogenisation in the ideological field. Obviously, economic globalisation does not triumph over differences, and it is not certain that it can reduce the variety of religions, languages, customs and tastes that constitute the many different indexes of identity. In fact, social identity is always communitarian, whether it knows it or not. The term gets bad press and communitarianism is denounced, but it is always the other's, for identity is produced in and by the social link.

Economic globalisation has not triumphed over these differences, but it has produced a new effect and specifically created neighbourhoods unheard of in history, composed of individuals of different cultures, with differentiated social identities – neighbourhoods that did not exist when "one did not mix", as Lacan puts it. From then on, there is a new worry which is expressed everywhere, that of the possible unity of this diversity. You are familiar with the values of the Republic that ought to be shared, the distinctive traits to be eradicated, veil or no veil, the problem of getting people to live together, of cohabiting, and also the problem of the reaction of nationalisms rising against this intermingling. We are in the midst of this configuration of mixing irreducible differences that capitalism does not order into a social link yet allows to exist side by side. The result is obvious: growth of hatred among neighbours, religious intolerance – to put it broadly, racism.

This is where segregation is convoked. It becomes the only mode for dealing with the differences between incompatible social identities now implanted on the same territory and implicated in the same economy. I say territory, but it is not an ethological problem; the management of spaces through separation of districts, partitioning, chosen or imposed, of living spaces and activitie, is today's last recourse for dealing with the experience of these incompatibilities. It is what I have called the solution by walls and as you know, for the one that fell in 1989, many others have been built, and not only in the Gaza Strip. Thus segregation echoes the new differences arising from the migratory flow, which are added to the old ones of social classes, with their inequalities and the disparity of their capital, not only financial but also cultural, "symbolic" as Bourdieu so well brings to light.

Currently, in our space of human rights, with our ideals of multiculturalism and respect for differences, we denounce segregation. This was not always the case. It was, as we know, fully legalised with regard to Blacks in America, for example, and not only legalised but justified and thought to be legitimate – which, by the way, verifies, if we still need to do this, that thinking is in sync with the discourse of the time. Today we try to counter segregation; just take a look at town politics, the architectural calculations to ensure social mixing, as they say. Why does this not work? Or at least works so badly that one can't help but notice how anti-segregationist ideals, which come from the "correct thinking" of our time, run aground on what is at the common root of segregation, itself subjective. Those who share the same convictions and the same bodily habits, in other words, homologous or related identities, get together, attract each other and thus separate from the others, separate from those who are "*apparolé*" to another discourse, who thus have other points of view about everything, or almost everything. Thus, segregation, far from being imposed, is being chosen, for example, when the upper-class districts resist public housing or in Latin America when the luxurious ghettos of the rich are sometimes protected by machine guns. Even more compelling, take the example of the very people professing anti-segregationist ideals and respect for differences yet lie with their behaviour, for to respect differences is not to love them, and this occurs at every level. Look at how tables are chosen at a group event, even one that is festive, and how the best-intentioned act, when it comes to choosing their lodging, their district and especially, especially, their children's school. There, correct thinking ends; the truth of the segregative option is out in the open. This is maybe why the most conservative classes make fun of the so-called bourgeois-bohemians *(bobos)*, for the latter always offer a pretty *(beau-bo)* discourse which, most of the time, their behavior does not confirm.

So then, where does the segregative option come from since languages, religions and cultures, in brief, have to mix? Lacan provides the key when he speaks, in *Télévision*, about the "racism of discourses in action". Discourses, as social links, order the jouissances, thus producing races of jouissance. The races, what we call races, are not a fact of nature but the fruit of discourse. Certainly, there are different skin colors and bodily characteristics on the planet, but when we say, for example, "the African man", this is a name that implies a multiplicity of discursive connotations, ultimately designating a heterogeneity of socially ordered jouissance. We could say the same thing about individual jouissance symptoms: they preside over affinities and detestations. We often hear from analysts that the symbolic alone can pacify these phenomena of rejection of the other and its difference. Is this the case? Not sure. Within a discourse, the semblant can give order; this is true. For example, it has allowed master and slave, men and women to coexist more or less in peace thanks to the "*apparolement*" of subjects, but it does not provide order between discourses; precisely the contrary: racism. At most, they can enlighten one another.

"Not all apparolé" to capitalism

I will end with this capitalist context. No doubt, the effects of capitalism make individuals insecure and not only at the level of work; capitalism makes social identities precarious and, as a consequence, increases identity fervour and inflames identity rivalries and racisms.

Question: what are the consequences for psychoanalysis?

Should we be alarmed, or should we have confidence in the future? Confidence, in fact, only has the value of what founds it. Lacan gives us an indication of this in *Télévision*. Freud said he had confidence in sexology, but this was a gratuitous confidence, in other words, not founded on knowledge. Lacan commented on this remark, saying, "It speaks volumes about his ethics". I asked myself about the following fact. With quasi-clairvoyance, Lacan, who was not especially optimistic, predicted much of what is happening under our eyes, notably the rise of segregation, racism, and also religion. Well, the very same Lacan who, in addition, produced the structure of capitalism, declared that he did not think capitalism's gadgets would prevail; in other words, that capitalism would succeed in making all of us entirely "*apparolés*" to its order. What could found such confidence if it did not come from a personal disposition to optimism? I have every reason to think it was based on his conception of the subject. The subject that speaks and that I have just called "*apparolé*" to the state of the social link, in order to say that it speaks the language proper to the discourse of its time and place, this subject is not all "*apparolé*" to the discourse; it is divided between what I attribute to its social identity and what is subtracted from this social identity. This division is not historical but structural, and it does not come from capitalism, which does not change anything about it.

Here, as a transition towards the question of the subject, a brief glance at Freud. In *Group Psychology and the Analysis of the Ego*, he rather insisted on the fact that the cohesion of the group, which, according to him, rests on two major types of identification, had the effect of modifying subjectivities. Notably, reducing ambivalence of feeling by fabricating "fraternity" between the members of the crowd, a feeling which generally gets good press; war films, especially American ones, are prolix on this point. The subject "*apparolé*" to the crowd pushes fraternity to its extremes. But Freud emphasised that this comes at the price of another change in individuals, namely the loss for each one of his specificity, let us say of his singularity of affects, but above all, his thinking. The crowd fabricates sameness at the cost of differences; it is a fashionable theme. Take note: this sameness is the kind of communitarian sameness that I call social identity. But if Freud emphasises the loss of identity in the crowd – by the way, the theme was already in the culture when Freud referred to it – it is precisely because, having discovered the unconscious, he had the idea of a possible singular identity, were it only by way of the unconscious desire proper to each one. All this to emphasise that the question of the link between identity and segregation can only be understood at the level of the identity of alienation, a social one, relative to a social link, for when it comes to a true identity, unique, if there is such a thing, the one I have called "of separation", it has no intrinsic link with the question of social segregation. However, it will introduce another problem, the opposite: that of knowing how the "scattered, ill-matched individuals" [*épars désassortis*] with their absolute difference maintain themselves in a social link.

Note

1 The word *apparolé* derives from Lacan's neologism *s'apparoler*, a combination of "*s'appareiller*" (to be coupled with and also apparatus) and "*parole*" (speech). Lacan used the neologism twice in his writings, first in 1969 in "*Préface à une thèse*" (Lacan, [1970] 1977, p. xi) and again in Seminar XVII, January 14, 1970 (Lacan, [1991] 2007, p. 51).

References

Baschet, J. (2014). *Adieux au capitalisme*. Paris: La Découverte.

Lacan, J. (1977 [1970]). Preface by Jacques Lacan. In: A. Lemaire, *Jacques Lacan*. D. Macey (Trans.). London: Routledge.

Lacan, J. (2007 [1991]). *The Seminar of Jacques Lacan, Book XVII: The Other Side of Psychoanalysis (1969–1970)*. R. Grigg (Trans.). New York: Norton.

Chapter 3

17th December 2014

I am going to address the question of identification from the analytic standpoint by way of considering the subject as redefined by Lacan. It is a subject whose identity is called into question – hence our difference with respect to the common problematics. But let me remind you, those we receive are not without identity [*ne sont pas des sans identités*]. On the contrary, they succumb to the identity indexes that are all the sexual, familial and professional coordinates that define one person in any given society, whether these coordinates place them on the side of the norm or the atypical. Currently, it is even noteworthy that identifying categories are made of what used to be formerly called symptoms or abnormalities. We thus have anorexics, suicidals, *Aspergers*, schizos, addicts, alcoholics, sundry junkies, and so on. Last time, I mentioned the tension, even the possible conflicts between the identity that is attributed to you by the Other, by the voices of all those others that can propound about you, and the identity awareness [*conscience propre d'identité*] that is, at times, not very self-assured. But in any case, the potential analysand who arrives is not someone without identity, and even more has a certain identity consciousness. Moreover, this is precisely why, in the beginning, it matters that it is put into question even though every psychotherapeutic intention aims at the opposite, that is to say, to ensure it, to reinforce it, even to make it acceptable, namely to resolve the so-called identity problems, uncertainties and conflicts.

Identity put into question

What can justify this analytic bias that questions identity certainties? In Freudian terms, one might say, nothing other than the unconscious, that guest which seems to inhabit you, that renders you incomprehensible to yourself and that produces all sorts of symptoms, behaviours and affects discordant with your intentions and your identity consciousness. From there, Lacan built his theory of the subject. It is new and does not designate the psychological subject of self-consciousness but that which results from the presence in him (the subject) of an unconscious which, only for him, of course, is a questioning of the identity he attributes to himself. What, then, is this subject redefined by Lacan that is so difficult to unglue from the

DOI: 10.4324/9781032645506-3

common definition of the subject? And if it is new, why keep the same term: subject? It is simple: when we say subject with Lacan, we designate the being insofar as it speaks; it is not the whole of the being because it first presents itself by way of its body, that is to say, its image. But the subject – the being insofar as it speaks then – includes in its definition both the subject of self-consciousness of the one who turns up, concerned with his own image and with his place in the world and who is coming to talk to you, and the subject said to be of the unconscious, supposed to the "it speaks" of the unconscious that produces symptoms, and which is yet unbeknownst to him. The so-called psychotherapies only know the first one, whereas psychoanalysis aims at the latter, although it is impossible to talk about a psychoanalytic treatment without convoking the subject of self-consciousness. This is the case when we speak about subjective rectification, which does not concern the unconscious per se. Likewise, when Freud speaks about "believing in the unconscious" or when one speaks about encountering one's unconscious, what is it but awareness? When one says: "I realised that. . ." it is not the subject of the unconscious that realises, and when Lacan sets down the duty for the analyst to think psychoanalysis, it is not the unconscious that is going to think it, etc. It is because the unconscious is language – thanks to Freud, who deciphered it as a language, although it is Lacan who formulated it this way – that the same term is used for the subject, in the banal sense of self-consciousness and also for the subject of the unconscious. It is majorly and primarily obvious for the said Lacanians who, let us notice, do not speak any longer about the ego, a term that translates the Freudian *Ich*, the first instance that he had opposed to the unconscious. Nowadays, we no longer measure the novelty, or even the shock, that this contribution of Lacan's once was. His construction of the subject starting from the unconscious language reformulates both Freud's second topic and what it replaced in Freud, namely his first construction distinguishing the ego and the repressed unconscious. Incidentally, right up to his last conference in Caracas in July of 1980, Lacan kept returning to the schema of this second topic.

Therefore, I am entering the theme of the subject.

The subject represented

The subject who speaks, conscious and unconscious, is represented by the chain of its articulated speech. Hence the well-known formula that presupposes the contribution of linguistics: "a signifier represents a subject for another signifier". Firstly, it is a thesis concerning the signifier; it is not as if he had said directly: a subject is what is represented by a signifier – even though he has also occasionally expressed it this way. What is proper to the signifier is to relate to other signifiers from which it is distinguished, and therefore because of that fact, it is tied (*solidaire*). It is the notion of the signifying chain:

$$\frac{S_1}{\mathcal{S}} \longrightarrow S_2$$

Its structure follows the pattern of an oriented binarity of the signifier, and Lacan spoke about an "ordered pair", one distinguished from the other. There is binarity, but one that is representative for the other; there is an orientation, an order. However, saying that it represents the subject, that is something else. It means that the signifier alone imposes a supposition of the subject defined as speaking. Hieroglyphics in the desert, so long as we do not mistake them for the effects of natural erosion, assure us that a subject was there. In other words: no signifier without another one or other ones, but no signifier either without a subject. This is the first thesis, and this is why, as soon as unconscious language is posed, namely the unconscious made of signifiers, we ask ourselves about the subject of the unconscious, namely the subject supposed to these signifiers. The question is explicitly formulated in "The Subversion of the Subject and the Dialectic of Desire".

What is this supposed subject? Indeed, the signifier does not say it; representing is neither qualifying nor identifying. Here, the signifier is nothing but a sort of delegate. Moreover, a delegate that is very quickly rejected because the slightest signifier causes (the subject) offense! This is what I informally evoked with: "I am not the one you think I am", where it comes down to a very general structure that cannot be reduced to the denunciation of appearances. In the signifying chain, the subject's being remains undetermined, so the represented is an undetermined, an x. For instance, Lacan says, explicitly about the dream, that language formation of the unconscious.

This problem exists for the Cartesian *cogito*, the one that is supposed to be thought. Descartes does not say signifier; he says thought, but the one that is supposed to be the "I think", if he does think and whatever he thinks, even if it is only thoughts of dreams, then his being is ensured. And he asks right away: "What am I then?" Descartes will answer: thinking substance. The representative does not identify, and what is represented can contest the representative. Incidentally, it is everyday life in a democracy, where citizens do have representatives that they contest. In psychoanalysis, the analysand also contests the representatives. For instance, he presents something that is equivalent to a signifier of the symptom, an S_1, or else some formations of the unconscious, his unconscious, emerge arbitrarily – dream, slip, that are thus S_1 – and he asks himself, if he is there, in what way does this represent him, and while asking himself about what it means, he looks for other signifiers that could give it sense. So, in his associative speech, while rectifying, while adding, he spends his time signifying, "that's not it". Lacan affirmed it: the subject "says no" to the signifiers because they offend it.

The subject that is represented is undetermined, but nonetheless, something of it can be ensured. Everything that can be known about it will bear the structure of the signifier. "What can I know? Reply: nothing in any case that doesn't have the structure of language" (Lacan, [1974] 1990, p. 36). Language does not say what the subject is, however, it imposes its conditions on it. In other words, its structure determines that of the subject, and it does so precisely: one signifier representative for the other or for some others; it then establishes a wrenching apart of these signifiers that Lacan called: "split subject" [*sujet refendu*]. As represented by language, it cannot be one, only a "certain two" [*quelque deux*]. In "Seminar XI", Lacan described a process of so-called alienation which seamlessly connects with the everyday clinic, the oscillation between the enigma of the S that emerged arbitrarily and the sense to be received. But none of these two poles have an identifying function. That the signifier represents the $ indicates precisely that it does not identify it. It is unfit for identity; it splits [*refend*] the subject, it condemns it to oscillate between petrification and sense and therefore cannot find any one-identity [*identité une*].

Moreover, the same question has to be applied to the image because the subject, defined as what is made present by language, is not the whole of the individual. First of all, this individual is represented, presented even, by his image and everything that goes together with it. Does the image identify it? Yes, but as early as the time of the mirror stage, which is only a first step, Lacan highlights the alienating aspect of the image of the ego in the mirror, a fixed image – that satisfies, that is libidinalised because it erects the form – but its fixity freezes and furthermore, being open to comparison, it introduces the register of aggressive competition proper to narcissism. And from here, Lacan even started to rethink the Freudian death drive. The thesis, therefore, was that of the image as a principle of misrecognition [*méconnaissance*]. We have to give full weight to this term: the subject, the one supposed to the signifier, cannot but misrecognise itself in its image, in the images constitutive of the ego. It is not for nothing that one of Lacan's first seminars was concerned with *The Ego in Freud's Theory and in the Technique of Psychoanalysis*, the main idea being that the subject can only be reached by moving aside the imagination of the ego. Thus the avoidance of the face-to-face position in the technique of analysis to deal only with the being who is addressing you, represented by what it actually says, the language of its associated statements, and also by what is deciphered in the Freudian practice. Lacan went as far as assigning to analysis and to the analyst a goal of the reduction of the ego, of the prestige of the images of the ego. It can be read very clearly in "Variations on the Standard Treatment" (Lacan, [1955] 2006), a text written to say that there is no typical treatment because there is no typical subject. Thus, the thesis of signifying alienation transposes a homologous thesis at the symbolic level. The signifier petrifies just like the image fixes except that the signifier itself can attribute sense. Hence an alternative that adheres to the analysand's phenomenology: either petrification or sense, but in both cases of this forced choice, there is a vacillation of identity. To the image as a principle of misrecognition, Lacan added the signifier as the principle of going astray. Hence the writing: $. These developments are useful in order to understand what Lacan writes in his short speech called "Peut-être à Vincennes" where he evokes the "average" analysts who only authorise themselves from their own going astray (Lacan, 1975 [2001], p. 314). The problem is thus the following: if the subject that is represented remains a supposed but undetermined presence, what then can sufficiently identify it in order to exit this straying?

The entrance of the subject into the real

In fact, everything I have just synthesised, and that is well-known to most, is only one side of the thesis.

The subject is not merely represented by language – we are not practising negative theology – it is also produced as an effect, a real effect of language that transforms the organism. This is the Lacanian hypothesis which is formulated at the end of *Encore* and which recalls how the so-called subject makes what Lacan calls in "Remarks on Daniel Lagache's Presentation" (Easter, 1960) its "entrance into the real" (Lacan, [1961] 2006, p. 548). This entrance is perceivable because the one supposed to speak, as undetermined as it may be, is not inert. It moves; it is "it" that speaks – thus, a dynamic principle. Where does this dynamism come from? It is produced from the encounter between language and what is not language, originally the vital need. This is what the first graph upon which Lacan has constructed his graph of desire and of the subversion of the subject writes.

This first graph shows that the organic being, written with the little triangle and whose pressure is represented by the retrograde arrow, once its pressure has passed through the signifying chain, becomes a subject, $. It passes through the chain of language as soon as the cry of need is converted into an articulated demand. This $, Lacan then places in the second graph where the organic being was in the first one, that is to say, at the beginning of the course of the retrograde chain which inscribed the pressure from need and which now inscribes what I have called the dynamism of the subject. This dynamism of the subject, namely of the being marked by the signifier, does not come from nature but from the effect of language, which is an effect of lack. I will not develop further this quite well-known thesis of the symbol as the killing of the thing, of the negativising effect of language illustrated by the *Fort-Da*. This lack pushes towards a quest – dynamism, then – and I might add towards some restorative quest. Furthermore, it inherits at least part of the pressure from the need because the body does not remain on the sidelines. It itself becomes subject to the drives that are substituted for the needs. When the cry of need is formulated into signifiers, as elementary as they may be, the being of the need becomes subject to the drive. The "Remarks on Daniel Lagache's Presentation"

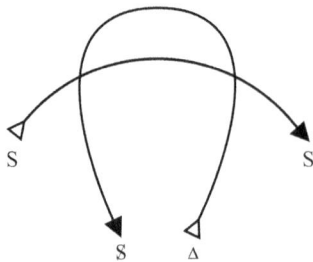

Figure 3.1 Graph 1

Source: Lacan ([1966] 2006, p. 681)

offers the corresponding formula: demand must be added to need "for the subject to make its entrance into the real, while need becomes drive" (Lacan, [1961] 2006, p. 548). The subject makes its entrance into the real not only as being supposed to the signifying chain but also as an effect of this chain that is not a chatter chain but rather the chain of the imperative demand addressed to the Other. Primary demand is, therefore, the origin of both the subject and the drive, and it is the real of prematurity at birth that is at the very foundation of its prevalence. At the same time as it is represented by the chain of its demand, the subject thereby makes its "entrance into the real" as libidinal pressure, an imperative whose entire question is to know what it is because, as represented, it remains undetermined.

The function of identifications

The graph of desire describes how the subject produced by the effect of language attempts to solve its indeterminacy by identifying itself. It is the process by which the one who speaks socialises himself, and it also indicates the function of identifications: those of the mirror stage summoned as a solution for the lack of unity, and those that pass through the signifier, whatever they may be, respond to the lack of identity. The range of their variety appears on the graph. I am thus going to spend some time on this graph. However, beforehand, in order to put things in perspective and not lose sight of the overall trajectory regarding the identity of the subject, let me highlight that Lacan, right after completing construction of his graph, which appeared in the 1958 article "Subversion of the Subject and the Dialectic of Desire", starts his seminar "The Ethics of Psychoanalysis" in autumn 1959 by taking up Freud's term: das Ding, the Thing, the other name of what speaks. Lacan defines this Thing: "it is the real inasmuch as it suffers from the signifier" [*pâtit du signifiant*] – again, in other terms, the Lacanian hypothesis – from the signifier that introduces there a void, a hole, a *nihil*, a gap (Lacan, [1986] 1992, p. 121) that presents us with its irreducible enigma. It is, therefore, that of the being that has become a subject that cannot be represented by the signifier. Suffice it to say none of the identifications previously listed in the graph has reduced its enigma.

I mentioned the function of these identifications: they are summoned by the lack of identity they plug up or rather dress up without managing to make a proper monk, recalling the proverb, "the cowl does not make the monk" [*l'habit ne fait pas le moine*]. Hence we can assign to analysis the following task, I quote Lacan, to "denounce" identifications. To denounce them is more than to list them; it is to highlight their failure as and when they are detected, namely their inability to saturate the question of "What am I?" Identifications fail on the question of identity, which is precisely the one at stake in a treatment. Hence the sometimes expressed concern about what is going to remain once the undressing is done, once the subject is laid bare. And indeed, as Lacan indicated, a treatment considerably increases the "destitution" of the subject. This is not to say that identifications cannot have positive functions – and one has to consider in what conditions and in what field – but, with respect to everything that can be ascribed to the real, identifications cannot but lie. This is particularly clear regarding sexuation. Man and woman are both signifiers that do not exist in nature, which knows only male and female. These are signifiers to which the various discourses attach specific postures, what we call femininity and masculinity, whose models are clearly cultural, subject to history and to successive fashions – here, fashion not only of clothing but more generally of customs which includes a distribution of all the specific social roles. Hence Freud's original idea in his Oedipus of the family, namely that one is adjusted to one's anatomical and legal sex thanks to a play of so-called oedipal identifications with the ideal images of the father and mother as paradigms for the man and woman. In this vein, Lacan at first followed Freud. I have said that the paternal metaphor was not a subversion of Oedipus, although, from the beginning, it stirred things up by substituting the identification with the phallus for the identification with the father and mother. Nevertheless, in both cases – Freud's Oedipus or Lacan's paternal metaphor – the solution to the question of sexual identity passed through the identification process or, in other words, through a semblant governing the pantomime of the sexes along with its inevitable social reach. These were two attempts to deal with the real of sex by means of the symbolic. At the moment of truth, however – an expression that, in fact, designates the time of the real in French when the bodies meet and when it is for real [*c'est pour de vrai*] as children say – we would like the act to have "some sexual pretences" (Lacan, [1974] 1990, p. 41). But it would require more than pretence for the subject to reach the Other during the act and . . . it fails, as we know all too well. None of the identifications that take shape on the wall of language gives a real solution to the real of "there is no sexual relation". Admittedly, one could possibly say that, after all, we give too much importance to this real of sex and that the well-organised semblants or even the theological virtues that Lacan evokes in "La Troisième" are better, but how can we treat with contempt a real, the one of the non-relation, which has subjective effects that disrupt links?

References

Lacan, J. (1990 [1974]). *Television: A Challenge to the Psychoanalytic Establishment.* J. Copjec (Ed.). D. Hollier, R. Krauss, A. Michelson and J. Mehlman (Trans.). New York: Norton.

Lacan, J. (1992 [1986]). *The Seminar of Jacques Lacan, Book VII: The Ethics of Psychoanalysis (1959–1960).* D. Porter (Trans.). New York: Norton.

Lacan, J. (2001 [1975]). Peut-être à Vincennes. In: *Autres écrits* (pp. 313–315). Paris: Éditions du Seuil.

Lacan, J. (2006 [1955]). Variations on the Standard Treatment. In: *Écrits: The First Complete Edition in English.* B. Fink (Trans.). New York: Norton.

Lacan, J. (2006 [1961]). Remarks on Daniel Lagache's Presentation: "Psychoanalysis and Personality Structure". In: *Écrits: The First Complete Edition in English.* B. Fink (Trans.). New York: Norton.

Lacan, J. (2006 [1966]). The Subversion of the Subject and the Dialectic of Desire in the Freudian Unconscious. In: *Écrits: The First Complete Edition in English.* B. Fink (Trans.). New York: Norton.

Chapter 4

7th January 2015

Thus I come to the question of identifications, our theme for the year, starting from the lack of identity of what we call subject. It (the subject) is an effect of language, as visualised in the first graph, indeed an effect that the signifier represents, but without being able to remove its indetermination, since this signifier imposes its own split [*refente*] on it (the subject). Basically, the subject is a being who has absorbed the Other's lack, that is, the negativising effect of language. From this, we grasp the general function of identifications: it is compensatory, although this compensation varies according to the types of identification since there are several types, and the question is to know if these types are ordered.

The order of identifications

In its structure, thus to be distinguished from its function, identification introduces two questions: With whom or with what does one identify, and by what? To the first question, there are many answers: with one's *semblable*, with the Other, but which one: the father, the mother, the leader, etc.? Putting them in order would not be excessive. As for "by what," we have various examples that are already known, i.e., by a trait, an image or a signifier; this is one of the definitions of the unary trait, but also by way of an affect, for example, in the participatory identification of the hysteric with the suffering of an other. In every case, it is a borrowing from some other, on occasion from its image, its subjective and/or social posture, but it is always partial.

To identify oneself has nothing to do with the mimetism well-known in the animal world, nor with imitation. Imitation, which is "doing the same as" at whatever level, voice, expression, posture, etc., nourishes those who speak the comic register of parody; this clearly marks its difference. Why does parody make us laugh? Maybe because it shows how much humans are caught up in the dimension of making semblance [*faire semblant*], all the way up to pantomime or, shall we say more generally, of appearing [*paraître*] whose mainspring is, in the end, precisely what Lacan called the semblant, that is, some signifier insofar as it engages something of the imaginary [*de l'imaginaire*], imagining itself or producing image effects. Nevertheless, the imitator is not changed by his imitation; once the performance is

DOI: 10.4324/9781032645506-4

over, he remains the same. An identification is something else: it borrows from the other, but it is a borrowing that is . . . constitutive according to Lacan's expression, that is, something that changes the identified. Sometimes the term "introjection" has been used; Lacan has commented on it a lot to emphasise that identification is not a surface phenomenon as imitation and mimetism can be. We know the formula, "I [*moi*] is an other" or even "I [*je*] is an other". Rimbaud made use of this.

It is nevertheless also certain that the change introduced by identification does not touch the whole of the identified being. The notion of tomboy expresses it quite well; one can borrow the silhouette, the typical behaviours, the tastes but . . . something does not stick, and that has to do with the reality of the body. *Tomboy*, for those who have seen the film, must come to realise this. This is what makes so strange, so problematic, for example, the talent of the actor who manages to incarnate the very presence of an other to the point of deception; even more problematic are the true simulators. But I return to the various identifications and what allows their ordering. This is what the graph of desire does.

Two primordial identifications

The graph of desire, the second written by Lacan, knots the two registers, that of the imaginary which he had introduced in "The Mirror Stage" and that of language, ascribed to the symbolic from the time of "The Function and Field of Speech and Language". This graph writes and orders two distinct identifications – both primordial – one imaginary, the other symbolic.

Following the retrograde vector, which starts from the $, we see that for it, the first identification is with the image of the small other; this is why we call it imaginary, the image that it encounters in the mirror or in the form of the little *semblable*. This

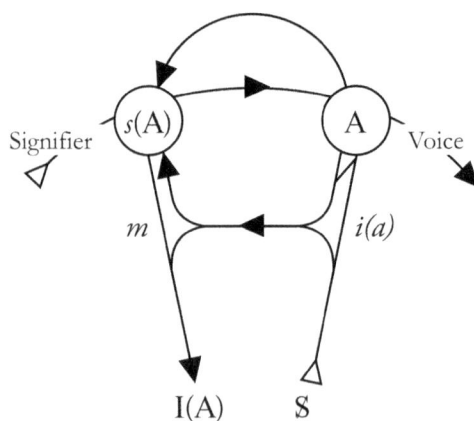

Figure 4.1 Graph 2

Source: Lacan ([1966b] 2006, p. 684)

image is constitutive of the ego, which is inseparable from this first identification by the image. It is written in the trajectory of the imaginary represented by the horizontal line, which goes from the i(a) to the ego, a trajectory traced below the signifying chain. I have called it 'first' but note, however, that it is second relative to the precedence of the appearance of the indeterminate $: non-identified, condition of all identification, and which itself is not without the signifying chain. Nonetheless, it is first in responding to this subject's lack. Here we have the question, remarked by all observers of young children, of the status of infantile transitivism, a type of induction by the animate image of the other, the little *semblable*, indeed a non-distinction between the ego and the other, which seems to precede the initial mastery of language but not, however, the effect of language with the first articulated demand. Concerning the function of this imaginary trajectory, we have clinical proof by way of the autistic child: having not entered the articulated demand, his body does not echo the saying of the Other's demand, nor has the $ made "its entrance into the real". He thus does not have the same relation to the mirror; he does not identify with the mirror image nor recognise himself in it; he is even persecuted by it.

This line of the first imaginary identification is not autonomous; it is written under the chain of the first demand in order to stress that the latter determines it as *a priori*. This is also emphasised by the two lines which converge on the ego, that of the retrograde vector which writes the movement issuing from the subject's lack and the one that comes from the Other via i(a). These lines show that the ego is dependent upon "subjectification by the signifier" (Lacan, [1966b] 2006, p. 685). Hence the idea, emphasised by Lacan for a very long time, of the subordination of the imaginary to the symbolic until it was put into question at the time of the Borromean knot. I have said that the graph knots the two registers, but take note, in a hierarchy, whereas the Borromean knot knots them without hierarchy. A big difference that makes the three registers autonomous and for which it would be necessary to determine the reasons and clinical consequences. But to do this, we probably need to move forward a bit more in the definition of the imaginary.

This second graph writes neither the chain of the unconscious nor the desire inscribed beyond the first chain of demand. The signifying chain is the chain of statements of the subject of self-consciousness, but it is a subject who speaks the Other's discourse, who receives its message from it, s(A), in an inverted form as Lacan expressed it, and who thus, first and foremost, receives its offers, which he will re-articulate in his speech, and to which his body will echo. This is the chain of the statements and transitive demands whose message relays the offer of the primordial Other, which is thus logically first articulated in oral and anal terms. This chain presides over an identification that Lacan qualifies as "primary identification" unknown to Freud, and written I(A). An identification, not with the image, but with the Other. Which Other? The one he posed as early as "Direction of the treatment and the Principles of Its Power", of the "mother's omnipotence" (Lacan, [1961] 2006, p. 517). Her power is the power of her speech, that of "the first words spoken" [*le dit premier*] which, and I quote, "legislate, aphorise, and are an oracle; they give the real other its obscure authority" (Lacan, [1966b] 2006, p. 684). I(A) writes "the assumption by the subject of the other's insignia" (Lacan, [1961] 2006, p. 525). Insignia: here, we have the partial trait of which I spoke. I call it unknown to Freud since we can see how much it differs from the first and obscure identification with the father that, according to Freud, precedes all libidinal investment and which presents its enigma ever since "The Ego and the Id". I will come back to this. Lacan convokes neither father nor mother, but the subordination to the chain of language and the first said [*le dit premier*]. It is conditioned by the dependence due to the immaturity at birth, thus a real, which situates the infant not only in a nursling dependence but also in dependence of language. In this sense, the symbolic itself is conditioned by the real. I(A) is the first symbolic identification of the subject, conditioning even its first imaginary identification. This can be written with the writing of the signifying representation of the subject: I(A)/$.

Obviously, this primordial structure is subsequently overdetermined by the effects of the chain of the unconscious; but let me emphasise how it allows us to grasp a large part of social phenomena, specifically of our time. Because the Other, this Other which determines the entire discourse of demand, which is tied to the value of images and ideals, is not only the familial Other; it is just as much the Other of social discourse from which each subject receives in part its own message, and which is a factor of "normalisation", that is to say, of the unification of behaviors, just as much as the first maternal demands. Of course, it is not fully sufficient; we can see what it lacks in order for it to account for the homogenising normativisation of the capitalist: the object as an effect of language is not yet placed there.

"The imaginary path"

It will be situated there once Lacan writes the line which goes from desire to fantasy. I emphasise that Lacan ascribes this line of desire to the imaginary, whereas generally, we put desire in the register of the symbolic. Having said that desire regulates itself on the fantasy [*se règle sur le fantasme*], he adds: "Thus closes the imaginary path, by which I must come into being in analysis, where the unconscious was (to be) *itself*" [*là où s'était l'inconscient*] (Lacan, [1966b] 2006, p. 691). He does not write *c'était* with a *c*, which would have evoked the *ça* [id], but with an *s*, the *s* of the subject. Why the imaginary path? We can already note that to introduce desire, Lacan does not write the complete graph. He produces his third graph, which situates desire starting from a double question mark coming from the Other, whose retrograde vector ends up with the fantasy, which he thus writes before writing the complete graph, as he calls it, on p. 692 of the *Écrits*, where the line of the unconscious appears. Why?

The $, the one represented by the first chain of demand and which has a relation with [*a rapport avec*] this Other of demand, encounters in this Other "something Other" (Lacan, [1966a] 2006, p. 710) than its transitive demand, because this Other, insofar as it is not only a locus of signifiers but an Other that speaks, is not less marked by language than the subject himself. It is thus inhabited by an indeterminate lack, an enigma, an *x*, "*Che vuoi?*" that we will call desire Å rather than

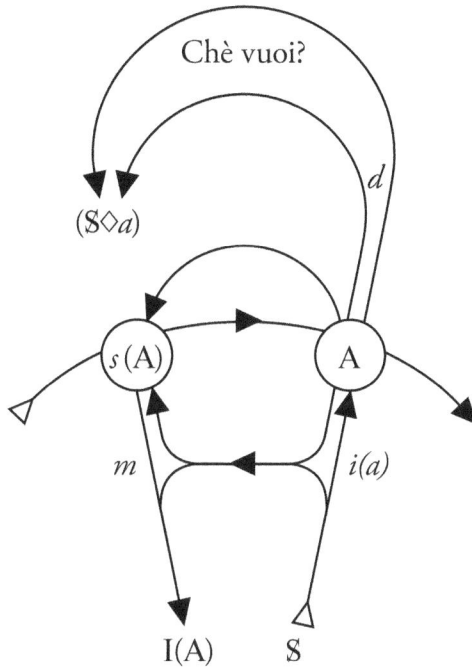

Figure 4.2 Graph 3
Source: Lacan ([1966b] 2006, p. 690)

omnipotence of subjection – sometimes even anguishing. And so Lacan goes on to write, before the final graph, the big question mark which comes from the Other.

Desire is encountered in the Other, the Other of speech, to the extent that speech conveys not only the oracles and explicit demands of the Other, but also what it does not say but can be implied, thanks to . . . the other chain of the unconscious, the one Freud would have called latent, repressed, and that the completed graph inscribes.

Desire going towards fantasy, represented by the horizontal line written between the two signifying chains, is, in fact, the signified of the upper chain of the unconscious, and this is why Lacan ascribes it to the imaginary because the imaginary is not reduced to the image. It is made of the signified-effects [*effets de signifié*] of language. Lacan made the linguistic subordination of the signified to the signifier, S/s, homologous to the subordination of the imaginary to the symbolic, S/I. Desire, which first presents itself in speech as an enigmatic signification is hence, as such, to be ascribed to the imaginary path. The forgery of the fantasy answers this enigma, and this is an "absolute signification", in other words, one which does not fluctuate because of other elements. We understand the rationale behind those two

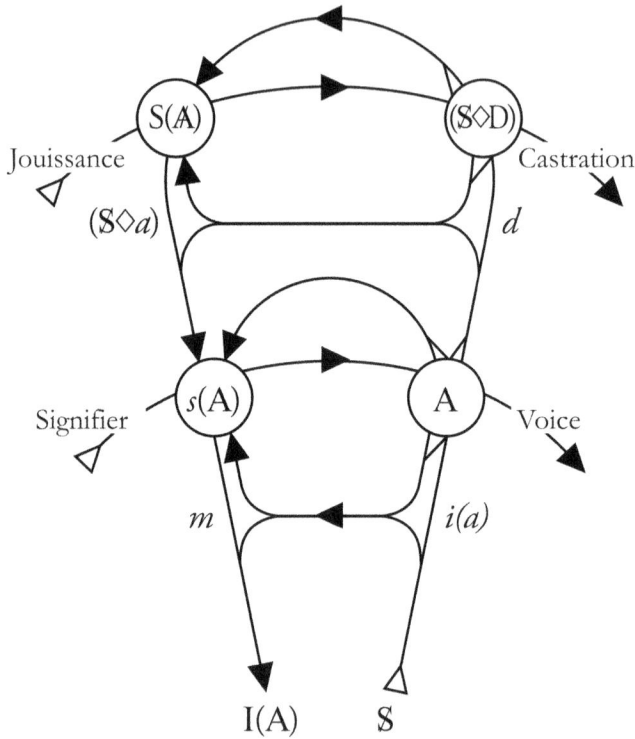

Figure 4.3 Completed graph
Source: Lacan ([1966b] 2006, p. 692)

graphs. The first one is about the experience, crucial for the one who speaks, of the encounter with the Other's desire and with the question it raises. The second one, with the line of the unconscious, gives the reason for this enigma of desire: it has to do with speech conveying the unconscious through metaphor and metonymy. We have to assess the scope and limits of this crucial phrase of Lacan: desire is the desire of the Other. In the objective meaning of "of" [*de*], it means that the Other is the object of desire; thus, that desire is desire of the Others's desire. Example: anorexia which can be a call for the Other's desire, which can carry a desire of the Other's desire when it is about force-feeding, in other words, when it is reduced to its demand. In the subjective meaning of "of" [*de*], it is the Other who desires; it is *qua* Other that the subject itself desires. What does it mean? It means that desire is linked to speech from the fact that it (the subject) speaks, it articulates another signifying chain, immanent, if I may say, to the chain of its statements. Through metaphor and metonymy, therefore, through the effect of language, its speech says of it much more than it knows, carries thus an unconscious enunciation, which has a signifier that Freud himself called unconscious desire. It is insofar as it is an effect of speech, an enigmatic effect because indeterminate, that desire is the Other's desire; in other words, it is insofar as it has no object that fixes it.

It is fantasy that fixes desire, giving it a determined form, but fantasy is that of the subject; it is of the Other only as fantasy about the Other, and it is as such that it sustains the desire of the subject as the desire of the Other in the objective sense of the "de". The imaginary path closes there by way of a second and specific imaginary identification. The first was that of the ego, written beginning with the preceding graph, to which is added that of fantasy, namely the identification of the supposed object of the Other's desire. It is "an identification of a strangely different kind" (Lacan, [1973] 1981, p. 257) from that of the unary trait [*Einziger Zug*] of the ego-ideal, I(A), said Lacan. This one comes to overdetermine both the message of the subject, s(A), and the first imaginary identifications of its ego, as shown by the retrograde vector, which is that of the subjectivisation of the subject as an effect of language. You should, therefore, not be surprised when you read in *On Freud's "Trieb"* that "identifications are determined by desire" (Lacan, [1964] 2006, p. 724), even though the first graph showed imaginary identifications of the ego determined by the primordial Other of the demand. There he can say "the identifications" without distinction since all are dependent on fantasy. The circle that closes the imaginary path is thus drawn; it includes the imaginary of the mirror that is overdetermined by that of the signification of desire.

We see the function of fantasy: it is a function of plugging up the subjective gap [*béance*] of the $. This was the case for the ego, as I already said, and it is also the case for fantasy. This is why Lacan evokes, in "Proposition of 1967", "the assurance" the subject derives from its fantasy. Indeed, the wanderer [*l'égaré*], the $ without identity, with his fantasy, which is an "absolute signification", that is to say, not split [*refendue*] by the signifier, this subject assures itself of its being as an object, it fixes his relation to the barred Other, A, just as his ego assured him of his fixed image. I have spoken of an imaginary circuit, but in fact, Lacan does not say circuit; he says path, which instead evokes a vector, the one drawn by the quest of the subject of lack. The so-called traversing of the fantasy is then the undermining of this assurance, its "vacillation", says Lacan, the destitution that I evoked last time. We sometimes hear it said that analysis reveals to the subject what he has been for the Other. This expression is very ambiguous; it allows one to think that fantasy is a stigmata from the real others of infantile history, whereas fantasy is a forgery that answers to the subject lacking identity, even if it draws on elements of its history.

Of course, it is not with his graph that Lacan said his last word about fantasy; he said more in his "*The Logic of the Fantasy*", but he did not say there that fantasy is real, only that it is in place of the real, hence the comparison to the function of a postulate in logic or mathematics, and also the recourse to topology in order to situate the two components of fantasy. The place of the real, what does it mean? If we retroactively apply the expression to the graph, the place of the real in the graph is where the Other is lacking, S(A), signifier of a lack in the Other, which says that the Other does not inscribe the jouissance. The graph does indeed inscribe an arrow, which goes from fantasy towards S(A̶) and designates the suppletive function of fantasy, which situates the object where the signifier is lacking. We can thus reformulate the phrase I quoted regarding the function of the imaginary path: there where it was [*s'était*], I come to be as . . . object *a* of the fantasy.

I will come back to the clinical examples with which Lacan has illustrated the thesis according to which identifications are determined from desire, even those which come directly from demand, for these are overdetermined and transformed by it. But for the moment, I would like to move on to an entirely different question.

An absence

Are you not astonished to note, and this is also how something emerged for me, that I could comment on the whole graph, all those mathemes, scrupulously following all of Lacan's own indications, and never encounter there what was at the heart of "The Direction of the Treatment", namely the phallic signifier, even though "The Direction of the Treatment" refers implicitly to the graph. Without it, there is no way to understand what Lacan formulated there when he said that desire is "beyond demand" and "in the [area] shy of demand". In the area shy of demand for love written in terms of drives on the upper line, beyond the transitive demands of the lower line. This is a direct reference to the topology of the graph that, nevertheless, he does not give in this text and in which, when he does give it, he does not write the phallus. Why? How are we to understand this?

References

Lacan, J. (1981 [1973]). *The Four Fundamental Concepts of Psychoanalysis, The Seminar of Jacques Lacan, Book XI*. A. Sheridan (Trans.). New York: Norton.

Lacan, J. (2006 [1961]). The Direction of the Treatment and the Principles of Its Power. In: *Écrits: The First Complete Edition in English*. B. Fink (Trans.). New York: Norton.

Lacan, J. (2006 [1964]). On Freud's "Trieb". In: *Écrits: The First Complete Edition in English*. B. Fink (Trans.). New York: Norton.

Lacan, J. (2006 [1966a]). Position of the Unconscious. In: *Écrits: The First Complete Edition in English*. B. Fink (Trans.). New York: Norton.

Lacan, J. (2006 [1966b]). The Subversion of the Subject and the Dialectic of Desire in the Freudian Unconscious. In: *Écrits: The First Complete Edition in English*. B. Fink (Trans.). New York: Norton.

Chapter 5

21st January 2015

So I left you with the question of knowing why identification with the phallus – on which Lacan insisted so much, starting from "On a Question Prior to Any Possible Treatment of Psychosis" up to "The Direction of the Treatment and the Principles of Its Power" together with "The Signification of the Phallus" – is not written in the graph, at least in a visible way. Now, those who have read these works know that he made of the phallus *the* signifier without peer, the signifier of the identification of the subject, and I quote: "the key to what we need to know in order to terminate our analyses" (Lacan, [1961] 2006, p. 526). Moreover, he added: "and no artifice can make up for it if we are to achieve this end". Consequently, it is a clearly stated "phallocentric" problem of the subject and of analysis. Is this elision motivated by a structural reason, or is it a theoretical reorientation?

Phallus, are you there?

First, I will situate the dates of the texts of reference. As I said, "The Direction of the Treatment" where the graph is implicit but not given, was written in July of 1958, six months after "On a Question Prior to Any Possible Treatment of Psychosis" which had laid the foundations for it by taking up the first two terms of the seminar on *The Psychoses*. "The Signification of the Phallus" is from the same year. The date when "The Subversion of the Subject and the Dialectic of Desire" was drafted, where he displays the graph, is not known for sure. The Congress of Royaumont took place in 1960, and the drafting of it was probably much later and certainly after "Kant with Sade", which is from 1962. Remarkably, this unique signifier that the two previous texts emphasise – as well as all the texts of Part V of the *Ecrits*, if you look at the table of contents – is not written in the graph, nor, for that matter, is the Name-of-the-Father, although the text dedicates several pages to the former and a few paragraphs to the latter. This is not to say that their function is necessarily elided. One might suppose that having completed its construction, Lacan takes it for granted as he often does. And let us not forget that this construction aimed at, among other things, rethinking the famous castration complex that Freud had situated at the origin of symptoms and subjective development, the paradoxes of which Lacan pointed out before attempting to explain them.

DOI: 10.4324/9781032645506-5

In fact, the question can be resolved if one examines the link between the identifications – the three identifications I have highlighted in the graph, namely with the image of the ego, with the ideal and with the object of the fantasy – thus the link between these identifications and the phallus. The formulation of the answer is, in fact, explicit from the time of "The Signification of the Phallus". After having defined what this term phallus connotes, Lacan adds: "that it can play its role only when veiled" (Lacan, [1966b] 2006, p. 581). Could it be in the graph but as veiled? The term is from the scopic register to indicate that it does not appear as such in clinical phenomena, more specifically in the scope of what is visible, and Lacan goes on to talk about its "disappearance". One can easily understand that the image of the penis is certainly not enough for it to appear. There is no doubt on that point in spite of certain Freudian equivocations, notably his confusion between the castration of the Mother and her absence of a penis.

But first of all, whence this veiling effect? From nowhere other than its own definition. It is well-known: it is not an object nor an organ but a signifier. It is the signifier that designates the effects of the signifier on the "*signifiable*" (Ibid., pp. 578–581). This term "*signifiable*" added as a third to the two terms already well-known since Saussure, namely signifier and signified, obviously designates a real to signify, first and foremost, the one that is written at the beginning of the retrograde vector of the first graph that I have discussed – said otherwise, what is living [*le vivant*] – that Lacan designates with the concrete term "need". The first and major effect of the signifier on this *signifiable* is, therefore $, the barred S. "The phallus", I quote, "is the privileged signifier of this mark" of the relation of the subject to the signifier (Ibid., p. 581). I have myself marked the bivalence of this effect that not only produces the subject but, in the same movement, also represses it – *Verdrängung* Lacan says – strikes it with "latency" according to the term used by Freud. The formula I started with, "the signifier represents the subject . . ." is a formula that implies this latency. I have developed it. It is written signifier/$, some kind of primary metaphor, an *Aufhebung* Lacan says, of which the phallus is the very signifier. How is this realised clinically? Lacan explained it: by means of the demand. We can therefore rewrite it D/d, the big D of demand whose effect is the subject of desire, written small d with the small letter of the signified, since desire is encountered as signified by means of demand and the phallus is thus its signifier at the same place in the graph. It is the writing of Freudian repression. One can find in Lacan several expressions: it is the signifier of the $, or the signifier of desire – it is the same thing – and he says interchangeably *Verdrängung* of desire or the phallus.

How to access what is veiled? The subject has access to it in the Other's place, where any signifier can appear. But I quote: "this signifier is there only as veiled and as ratio [*raison*] of the Other's desire, it is the Other's desire as such that the subject is required to recognise" (Ibid., p. 581–582). One cannot encounter the phallus but can encounter desire, namely the Other, as "a subject divided by the signifying *Spaltung*" (Ibid., p. 582). Here is the reason behind the intermediate graph with its question mark that provided the path of access to this invisible phallus.

So, what does appear there where the phallus does not? Firstly, the x of desire, the enigma of the Other, but that is not all. Identifications also appear – I remind you of what I have already indicated – identifications that are "determined by desire". The most convincing illustration of this structure is located at the level of the relation between the sexes. The repression of the x of desire shifts all sexed manifestations into the "seeming" [paraître]. For lack of knowing what desire aims at, the object that it targets, we convoke the images and ideals, namely the imaginary identifications of the ideal ego, that is to say, the ego conceived as lovable, and the symbolic identifications of I(A) that Freud called ego-ideal. These are written on the graph, and I went over it last time. It is they that have a veiling function. What gives credit to these images and ideals is that they are suitable for satisfying the demand for love. Therefore one gives oneself some airs of sex, some airs of man, virile display, and some airs of woman, feminine masquerade, in order to be what the Other is lacking.

From my point of view, that is what justifies the fact that Lacan has used the term veil, which is a term from the imaginary register, in order to state the repressed presence, that Verdrängung of desire or of the phallus that comes from the signifying effect and which is not imaginary. It is difficult to think that it was only because the veil was present in the mysteries of the ancients that Lacan, following Freud, evoked it. But the term veil is more easily understood once we realise that identifications, both imaginary ones of the ego and symbolic ones of the subject that appear in visible phenomena, veil what is their reason, their mainspring, the phallus. The "seeming" [paraître] represses the being of the lack of desire, namely the phallus. To use an analogy: Mr. Muscle – whether or not this muscle is a metaphor – is not to be confused with Mr. Phallus or desire. Mr. Muscle only shows his muscles in order to seduce the Other – which is why, oddly enough, virile display feminises, Lacan says. The secret of that mask that appears in what is visible is the phallus insofar as it is the reason for desire. It is desire as the desire of/for [de] the Other, desire of/for its desire under the cover of the demand for love. We can thus write this covering of the Verdrängung of the phallus:

$$I(A) - \frac{MI}{\varphi}$$

So, the assaults on the imaginary, the visible marks of the deficit in the image, or the uncertainties of adhering to the semblants of the ideals can take on a signification of lack, even of castration. The example of the little girl who develops a phobia, commented on by Lacan – the phobia being a symptom of defence against maternal castration – makes much of the fact that she saw her Mother in a poor state, ill and plodding along heavily. These imaginary appearances that make some difficulties of the Mother visible, that show her without muscles, if I may say, in order to prolong my example, come to represent (the imaginary veil again) another difficulty, another defect at the level of desire. Moreover, in clinical work with young children, the moment when the absence of a visible penis takes on this signification which is both questioning and distressing is very much noticeable.

Let me conclude the question I previously posed. Although the phallus is not written in the graph, it is nonetheless present but as veiled, which is its status. The graph does not elide its function, that which the phrase I have quoted calls its role. I will return to this function, but first, let me pause a moment on another question I have been working on for quite some time. Is this signifier solidary with the function of the Father? All those who have read Lacan know that it is what he postulated at first in "On a Question Preliminary to any Possible Treatment of Psychosis". I will go into the details later on.

Genealogy of the phallus

Firstly, I would like to show that, if we follow the texts, we can see, not only that Lacan did not write the phallus in the graph, neither the small one nor the big one, which can be explained as I have just described, but also that the two notations he uses – small φ and capital Φ – to situate the phallic register in "Subversion of the Subject and the Dialectic of Desire", he introduces them and comments on them without any reference to the Father, setting up for the phallus from this text onwards some sort of genealogy without the Father. In re-reading "The Signification of the Phallus" in order to date this, I realised that it was already the case. I am going to make an inventory of the various developments which attest to this.

"The Signification of the Phallus" is an essential text. First of all, Lacan clarifies in it the status of the phallus as a signifier, then its function in the relationship to the Other, and he even questions its origin, I mean the way it was "chosen", that is his term, all of this without passing through the mediation of the Father. One sentence only is dedicated to the latter in a passage to which I am drawing attention (Ibid., p. 581–583). Firstly, Lacan reformulates the so-called castration complex as "the test constituted by the Other's desire" in so far as the subject "learns that his mother does not have it" (Ibid. p. 582) – the phallus – with all the symptomatic and structural consequences indicated by Freud. Obviously, this poses the question of what it means to not have the phallus, but I am only highlighting for now what he subsequently specifies, and in a very small sentence, that the future of this sequence of the castration complex will, of course, depend on the law of the Father. We thus have a castration complex that does not include the Father, who is nonetheless expected in the aftermath. One cannot state more clearly the autonomy of the phallic register and that the Father is not the castrator, which "Subversion of the Subject and the Dialectic of Desire" explains without ambiguity while further accentuating the theme up to the famous formula stating that the Oedipal show "cannot run indefinitely". These are neither empty nor vague words.

Where does this newly readable autonomy come from? I think it logically stems from the specifications brought to the definition of the phallus. In "On a Question Preliminary to any Possible Treatment of Psychosis", this phallus taken from Freud was evoked by Lacan in the R schema as a "phallic image" and then as a signifier of the imaginary object of the Other, the Mother, and he claimed that it could be evoked in the imaginary of the subject, thus as a signification, only by means of a metaphor, the paternal one. There was a subtlety here to be laid out because this construction indicated that this signifier present in the Other may not have been operating for the subject. Incidentally, in the metaphor, the Mother's desire (DM) does not write the desire proper to the Mother. What it writes is the desire that her absence symbolises . . . for the child, the operation of symbolisation thus operating on the child's side. "The Signification of the Phallus" aims at clarifying its definition, which indicates clearly the presence of a question. He posits it, as I said, as the signifier of the effects of the signifier on the signifiable (cf. Lacan's hypothesis); the signifiable that the signifier stamps with its bar, with the $ the result. Consequently, this phallus connotes both the linguistic negativisation featured by the bar – which is why Lacan always links death with the signifying sequence – and what remains of vital energy, of dynamism for the subject, and this is named desire, life "supported by death" he says somewhere, death that is conveyed by language. Defined in this way, how could it be lacking in any subject since the subject is the effect of this bar?

This argument is redoubled in the same text by means of a genealogy of desire (Ibid., p. 579) that originates primarily between need and demand. Needs are alienated in demand; the particularity of what they demand is cancelled by the demand for love that bears on something other than the satisfactions, namely the presence or the absence of the Other. According to Lacan, the part of needs that thus falls in the *Urverdrängung* reappears in desire, beyond and below demand, and as the "power of pure loss". Here is a genesis of desire that does not pass through the function of the Father. Moreover, it is interesting to observe that Freud, at the end of *The Interpretation of Dreams*, also tried to develop such a structural genesis of desire based on the first experience of satisfaction. So, are we going to continue to say that there is no desire and no phallus if there is no paternal metaphor?

Furthermore, Lacan poses the question: why was the image of the penis chosen – it is the term used by Lacan – as a symbol when the ancients called it a simulacrum? Lacan often revisited the question and not for nothing, in "The Signification of the Phallus", in "Subversion of the Subject and the Dialectic of Desire", once again in "L'étourdit", and he answers it by using various arguments but none that convoke the Father. He evokes the characteristics of the organ, its position as a pointy extremity on the surface of the body and its erectility "concentrating in itself the most intimate aspect of autoeroticism" (Lacan, [1966c] 2006, p. 696) that makes the prototype of the detachable object out of it, the fact that it is missing in the specular image. . . . The thesis is resumed in "L'étourdit" in very similar terms – see the paragraph in the middle of page 692 (Lacan, 1973). It is, therefore, not chosen as an effect of the Father, and, incidentally, it is also necessary to suppose it in order to account for the fact that the universality of that phallic symbol, confirmed by the entire ethnology, is much more indisputable than that of the much contested Oedipus complex.

Even more important is the fact that Lacan explicitly reverses the common idea, derived from the metaphor, of the relation between desire and Law. He writes "Law" with a capital letter, and when we say Law with a capital letter, we think of

Freud and the function of the murder of the Father in the prohibition of incest. This is the law concerning the limitation of jouissance by means of the subtraction of the first object. Well, far from desire originating from the Law, that is to say from the prohibition, from any prohibition that would be founding as some may say, I quote: "But I will stop here again in order to return to the status of desire, which presents itself as independent of the Law's mediation, because Law originates in desire" (Lacan, [1966c] 2006, p. 689). It is categorical if we read it well. He specifies: desire, far from proceeding from the prohibition [*interdit*], imposes itself as an "absolute condition" and imposes itself structurally from the effects of demand upon need. "Absolute condition" means "detachment"; it is his own term, detachment not only from need but also emancipation from the subjection to the Other that the demand for love maintains. Thus, a double detachment. But "absolute" also says "without concession" and the virulences that do not compromise. According to Lacan, the transitional object, the separator, is clinical testimony to that precocious and structural dimension of desire and to its function. And Lacan adds the following sentence that I introduce for your examination: "This is, frankly, no more than an emblem; representation's representative in the absolute condition is in its proper place in the unconscious, where it causes desire" (Ibid., p. 689), etc. Representation's representative is the term that Lacan always uses for the signifiers of the unconscious. Here, it can only be the signifier said [*dit*] of desire, the phallic signifier. How better to say that it does not need the Father to inscribe itself in it?

And for confirmation, take a look at the end of the text, where it deals with jouissance: "it is not the Law itself that bars the subject's access to jouissance" (Ibid., p. 696), it is . . . speech. "Jouissance is prohibited [*interdite*] to whoever speaks, as such" (Ibid., p. 696); in other words, castration of jouissance by the effect of the signifier but what remains is the jouissance said [*dite*] between the lines, *inter-dite* with a dash, this one being impossible to negativise. The one missing and the one remaining are both effects of language. In *Le Sinthome*, Lacan dots the i's and crosses the t's. I have quoted him when he says that phallic jouissance is a result of speech and its encounter with the body. Nevertheless, we can see that the thesis of an effect of speech already separated from the function of the Father was clearly explicit in "Subversion of the subject and the dialectic of desire" and "The Signification of the Phallus". Besides, did he not say that the Law transmitted by Moses was nothing but the laws of speech? What does it mean? That it was nothing but a structural necessity which thus makes the prohibition appear, carried by a prohibitor, like a myth rationalising the impossible. The impossible secretes the fictions that would justify it. This is what myth is. *Télévision* dots all the i's on this subject, but I will not develop this further.

I am surprised today that all of this, perfectly articulated since that time, has not been enough to call into question the discourse derived from the paternal metaphor, a discourse that still matters to some and according to which there is no phallic register without the Father.

This genealogy of the phallus without the Father already present in "Subversion of the Subject and the Dialectic of Desire" can be refound in ". . . or Worse" and in

"L'étourdit" where the phallic function is introduced without passing through the Father, as a function of speech; I have already insisted on this. Suffice it to say that when re-reading Lacan, one realises that on that point, it was not necessary to wait for his final teaching, not even "Radiophonie" where as early as 1970, he explains his "no recourse to the Name-of-the-Father" in order to understand that he had gone beyond the Oedipus complex.

What is at stake in the question is not paltry. Like any theoretical reworking, this one imposes some obligations of adjustment; here, that of the very conception of psychosis itself since, from the beginning, he had entirely conceived it as resulting from the metaphor that is lacking, the metaphor which postulated the operation of phallicisation of the lack as passing through the Father, from which we kept on re-peating: no phallic signification in psychosis due to foreclosure of the Father, hence no castration and therefore . . . no desire. There, everything has to be redone. Incidentally, Lacan paved the way: he gave certain indications, but they are scattered and not systematised. For example, that S, S_1, S_i and a are all valid for psychosis which does not prevent most people today from taking for granted, with no further questioning, that the phallic function is not present there. Indeed, the question is very difficult, and I will try to get back to it insofar as I can, but I still remain on the phallocentric clinic for now. It begins in Freud with the function that he attributes to the castration complex for both sexes, and it produced some memorable writing from the pen of Lacan.

The phallocentric clinic

It is not excessive to say that this role of the phallus is copulatory. For the moment, I am not talking about the copulation between two bodies but between the subject and the Other. To begin with, Lacan put emphasis on this aspect more than on the sexual function. This copula is, therefore, at stake at different levels: between the child and the Mother, between the neurotic and his Other, and also between lovers insofar as the subject is there. Indeed, as long as it is the signifier of both the subject's lack and that of the Other, the way is paved for an articulation between these two lacks, specifically a dialectical identification with the Other's lack of which the phallus is the signifier. Hence the formula: "identification with the phallus", that is to say, identification with what is lacking in the Other. To the question of the undetermined subject: "What am I?", this identification attempts to bring the answer into existence: I am the lack in the Other. Only, being the lack in the Other is the wish that drives the demand for love, which actually requires the Other to give its lack, but under this demand, there is the desire of/for its desire. Lacan says it when it comes to the relationship of the child with the Mother: "a relationship that is constituted in analysis not by the child's biological dependence, but by its dependence on her love, that is, by its desire for her desire" (Lacan, [1959] 2006, pp. 462–463). Incidentally, we have in this sentence a definition of the link between the intransitive demand for love – the one written on the right part of the upper line of the graph – and the desire for desire that is the signified of it. It is with this same construction that Lacan situates the function of the analyst's desire as, I quote, "The true and final mainspring of what constitutes transference" (Lacan, [1966a] 2006, p. 716), as demand for love. But this sentence also carries a problem. How do things arrange themselves at the sexual level, given that desire and love have the same signifier, the phallus? The first answer given by Lacan, which is very well-known by his readers, is the following: love is to want to "be" the phallus. It is therefore convoked here from the point of view of the question of identity, of what am I? Desire as being not only desire for desire, the desire of the Other, but transitive desire, if I may say, desire with an object, possibly a sexual one, it requires the activation of the phallus as possession, instrument.

References

Lacan, J. (2001 [1973]). L'étourdit. In: *Autres écrits* (pp. 449–498). Paris: Éditions du Seuil.

Lacan, J. (2006 [1959]). On a Question Prior to Any Possible Treatment of Psychosis. In: *Écrits: The First Complete Edition in English*. B. Fink (Trans.). New York: Norton.

Lacan, J. (2006 [1961]). The Direction of the Treatment and the Principles of Its Power. In: *Écrits: The First Complete Edition in English*. B. Fink (Trans.). New York: Norton.

Lacan, J. (2006 [1966a]). Position of the Unconscious. In: *Écrits: The First Complete Edition in English*. B. Fink (Trans.). New York: Norton.

Lacan, J. (2006 [1966b]). The Signification of the Phallus. In: *Écrits: The First Complete Edition in English*. B. Fink (Trans.). New York: Norton.

Lacan, J. (2006 [1966c]). The Subversion of the Subject and the Dialectic of Desire in the Freudian Unconscious. In: *Écrits: The First Complete Edition in English*. B. Fink (Trans.). New York: Norton.

Chapter 6

4th February 2015

I previously mentioned an example of the first copulatory function of the phallus. I am borrowing it from Lacan in "The Direction of the Treatment". This example is paradigmatic, the one of that witty hysteric whose dream Freud recounts in *The Interpretation of Dreams* and whose case Lacan discusses in "The Direction of the Treatment". The example is paradigmatic for three reasons: not only because it gives the structure of hysteria itself, but also because it illustrates the thesis of the phallus, which is veiled by the identifications both imaginary and symbolic, and finally, because it displays how the phallus, just like desire, "is its interpretation". Furthermore, the development that Lacan gives to it is a masterly example of deciphering and interpreting a dream.

Socialising phallus

I am condensing the example that I previously developed in detail (Soler, 2006, pp. 49–59). Freud tells us that this young woman identifies with her friend. It is thus an identification on the imaginary axis a/a'. The trait that marks the identification is the signifier "caviar" because she treats it in the same way as her friend treats the salmon, a friend who says she desires it but denies it to herself. And Freud comments: a desire for unsatisfied desire. Obviously, it is here a question of preconscious desires, implied by her speech and her daily behaviour with her beloved husband, that makes her a "woman who is fulfilled". "One still must go further to figure out what such a desire means in the unconscious" (Lacan, [1961] 2006, p. 519). Here are clearly articulated the two registers of the preconscious and the unconscious to be interpreted. Lacan formulates it thus: "If our patient identifies with her friend, it is insofar as she is inimitable" (Ibid., p. 522). In other words, we do not know what she wants nor what she is aiming at through this scenario of the salmon. The imaginary identification is thus itself overdetermined by the question of desire. Then, the analysis of the dream, which I will not take up here, allows us to move towards another identification because, behind this dream, there is the question of the subject concerning the desire of the Other – upper case – here the husband, the earthy butcher who always speaks well of the friend, this scrawny one, whereas he enjoys and satisfies himself with curves. Wherefrom

DOI: 10.4324/9781032645506-6

Lacan extracts the question of the subject: how can a man love a woman when he cannot be satisfied by her? It is precisely the question of hysterical identification, a question which clearly has to do only with desire, here the desire that remains in the Other when everything else in it is satisfied, desire insofar as no jouissance can satiate it. Represented by this question, the subject – here the woman – identifies itself with the Other – here the man – a symbolic identification this time with desire as lack and not with jouissance, the lack being represented in the dream by the single small slice of salmon with which one cannot give a dinner. So where is the phallus? It is veiled by the identification of the subject with the lack of the Other, which presides over the imaginary identification with the friend. It is veiled and remains as such if the interpretation does not lift the veil in order to formulate the unconscious wish. Hence the formula: "desire is its interpretation". And this is also true for what Lacan called the child's encounter with the desire of the Other. Indeed, what the Other does not say, but that reveals itself between the lines or in the holes of its discourse, is not questioned as desire without a subjective act, and it is the reason why I spoke about the interpreting child [*enfant interprète*]; the so-called cases of "as-if" personalities are precisely cases of non-interpreting subjects. So in the case of the beautiful butcher's wife, the interpretation is formulated: "to be the phallus", the signifier of desire. And Lacan humorously adds: "even a somewhat skinny one", precisely to say that the phallic signifier is covered by the somewhat scrawny image that is veiling it. He comments: "Isn't that the final identification with the signifier of desire?" Final because it is the last one that we challenge in the end after having listed the signifiers and the images that are veiling it. But it is not chronologically final; rather, it is first because this dialectic starts early with the encounter with the desire of the Other. This example shows us the phallus in what I will call its socialising function, and it is not by chance if, several years later, Lacan makes of hysteria a type of social link.

Parenthesis: this analysis of the beautiful butcher's wife's dream is a masterly demonstration of how deciphering a dream enables the interpretation of desire, and it is also a paradigmatic illustration – this is how Lacan described it – of the clinical structure of hysteria. Throughout the years and until the end of his teaching, Lacan developed it but without ever calling into question that first thesis of a structure identified with and by the desire, and not with jouissance, a structure that is a desire of/for desire. Lacan reaffirmed it with all the following well-known expressions: she does not know that she would like to leave her butcher of a husband to another woman; the hysteric goes on a strike of the body; she falls under the ethic of "outside sex" [*Hors Sexe*]; it is a discourse; she is not the ultimate symptom as a woman can be, etc. Nevertheless, to no avail, many continue to say, in the name of Lacan and in spite of him, that this structure is defined by the primacy of the jouissance of sex. In any case, what is certain is that the core of every neurosis is hysterical.

"The Direction of the Treatment" ends with the assertion about the neurotic, which states that "his desire is to be it", the phallus. Yet, according to Lacan, "being the phallus" is the very formula of the demand for love. This is not an inconsistency because the demand for love, like any demand, carries a desire, but not just any desire; it carries desire as desire of the Other, in the objective sense of the "of", that is to say, desire for its desire. The desire for desire, is a pure desire; I mean a desire without an object, or a desire within which desire has become an object. Lacan reiterates this in 1973 in "*L'introduction à l'édition allemande des Écrits*", concerning the "hysteric's discourse", referring to the beautiful butcher's wife, he writes: "What is at play for them [male or female] in identification is structure and not meaning, as is clearly read in the fact that it bears on desire, that is to say, the lack taken as an object and not the cause of the lack" (Lacan, [1973] 2001, p. 557). We can see here that hysteria isolates one of the two possible articulations of desire. It is not desire insofar as it aims at a substantial object but rather desire insofar as it aims at the Other. With this structure, one can understand the sentence from "The Subversion of the Subject and the Dialectic of Desire" which many wonder about; the one that says that "the neurotic, whether hysteric, obsessive, or, more radically, phobic is the one who identifies the Other's lack with the Other's demand" (Lacan, [1966b] 2006, p. 698), D, implicitly not with its jouissance, Φ. We can understand it if we unfold this big D: to be the phallus; it is the formula of the demand for love which carries and has as signified the desire of desire.

$$D : \text{"To be the phallus"} = \frac{\text{Demand for love}}{\text{Desire of desire}}$$

This phallus as signifier of the demand for love that carries the desire of desire is at the heart of the three passions of being: love, hate and ignorance, which are based on the lack in being [*manque à être*]. Nevertheless, the signifier of desire is not written with an uppercase letter. "The Subversion of the Subject and the Dialectic of Desire" adds two notations to it: the -φ and the uppercase Φ. This change comes from a problem that Lacan encountered in its construction.

Two lacks

The lack in being [*manque à être*] is, after all, not the lack in enjoying [*manque à jouir*], which is a totally different thing. When Freud talks about the phallus and about castration, for him, since the beginning, it is the organ of sexual jouissance and the threat cast on it [*sexual jouissance*]. What justifies Lacan in making it the signifier of the lack in being and the signifier of the lack in enjoying? How does the transition from the lack in being to the lack in enjoying – a transition that Freud's word "castration" designates – occur? In any case, this transition is indicated by Lacan himself. Right after he is finished with the butcher's wife, there is a paragraph about the castration complex and penis envy.

Demand in itself bears a signification of lack. What would there be to demand if not for a lack, whatever it might be? It is moreover certain that the field of appetencies is not reduced to sexual desire, far from it. We could write the lack involved in demand with a -1 in the place of the signified: D/(-1), (-1) inscribing the signification of an undetermined lack. In a way, this lack is subdivided into lack in being and lack in enjoying. The lack in being falls in the category of the identity questions generated by the signifying representation of the subject, and it addresses the Other, specifically in the demand for love. The lack in enjoying falls in the category of the effects of language [*langage*] on need, with the loss it produces in it, and it implies the body of drives [*corps pulsionnel*]. Firstly, Lacan has insisted from the beginning on the lack in being, probably because his contemporaries had already started to take as a compass the exigencies of the demand. "The Direction of the Treatment" and also "The Signification of the Phallus" insist on this problem of the lack in being and what can heal it, or at least compensate for it in love – although in the case of the three-card monte man, Lacan attempts to link it to actual sexual activity and desire. But one cannot say that this is totally convincing, contrary to the case of the butcher's wife. Yet it is on the basis of this so-called phallic identification with the Other's lack in being that Lacan is obliged to make the link with Freud's theses on castration which is always formulated in terms of having the organ or not. "The Signification of the Phallus" tries to articulate this in the very definition of the castration complex that ends with this statement: it shows "the conjunction of desire, insofar as the phallic signifier is its mark, with the threat of or nostalgia based on not-having" [*manque à avoir*] (Lacan, [1966a] 2006, p. 582). Conjunction. What does this so-called complex conjoin? The lack in being of the demand for love, which bears the desire for desire, D/d, and the not-having of the organ of jouissance. As he unfolds his hypothesis regarding the effect of language – I have myself commented on it – Lacan affirms that this effect, the one of the first demand as articulated, is double, namely $barred{S}$ and the drives; on one hand, the barred S of the lack in being and of desire, and on the other hand, the drives whose activity is of jouissance, the jouissance triggered by the lack in enjoying produced by the effect of language on needs – the Lacanian hypothesis.

Lacan writes these two effects in "The Subversion of the Subject and the Dialectic of Desire" by splitting into two the phallic signifier and by writing both (-φ) and Φ. Note that hitherto the phallus, in the demand for love with the formula "being the phallus", was not written minus phi (-φ). This is because the lack in being cannot be quantified, it can be experienced more or less, but it does not lend itself to arithmetic, to the plus or the minus. And in love, when each gives and receives what he does not have, the phallus is positivised, and there is reciprocity. But in the act of jouissance, it is something else; one gives what he has, and the other receives it. It is an irreducible disparity that duplicates the anatomical disparity. So in "The Subversion of the Subject and the Dialectic of Desire", one can notice that the emphasis is no longer on the identifying function of the phallus, on "being the phallus", but on castration, "which is not a myth", and on the question of jouissance. He goes on to write the lack in being with the (-φ), which is the imaginary function of castration, to which he adds the big Φ, signifier of the jouissance, that which remains. It is a considerable addition. Where to put them on the graph? If one had to do it – Lacan did not do it, but he gave some indications – he would put the (-φ) on the line that goes from desire to fantasy, precisely the line that closes the imaginary path. Indeed, Lacan insists here (-φ) is implicit in both terms of the fantasy, and he illustrates it with the couple Alcibiades/Socrates. As for Φ, it is at the same place as S(A̸), "in the privileged place of jouissance" that fails to be inscribed in the Other.

I will return to this point. What is important for our question of identifications is that this phallic register, which is implicit in the graph, reverberates on the identifications which I spoke about at the beginning, the ones he called imaginary identifications in fantasy and of the ego, and the symbolic one of the I(A), because all of them are dependent on the unconscious upper chain and are modified by it. It is thus that the big Φ and drive objects have an impact on the imaginary fantasy, which is represented in the graph by the various arrows. As for the I(A), the ideal of the Other that in the second graph was firstly tantamount to the identification with the total power of the Other, it becomes the identification with the barred Other, that is to say, to the inconsistent Other of the upper line which is in solidarity with (-φ) on the line of desire. So, in the aftermath, in *Télévision*, Lacan is able to complete his idea about feminine masquerade. As I have said, up to this point, he had indicated that it is situated in the seeming [*paraître*], let us say in the making semblance [*faire semblant*] of the ideals of sex proper to satisfying the demand for love – these are his words. From now on, he says that it is no longer "the falsehood that some ingrates" impute to it. This means that it is not only at the level of a phallicised, agalmatised [*agalmatisé*] seeming; it has a function even down to the sexual act itself, that of satisfying or, we wish to say, luring the masculine fantasy, enough to ensure its jouissance. Now we are no longer in the previously evoked area of reciprocity between parade and masquerade.

Let me conclude with the question that I posed. Although it is not written per se, the phallic register is undoubtedly included in the graph and even completed by the signifier of jouissance to a great extent.

And the Name-of-the-Father?

I can ask about the Name-of-the-Father the same question I asked about the phallus: Father, are you there? The phallus is. Does it imply that the Name-of-the-Father is there? I mean, that it is located in the unconscious, as apparently posited in "On a Question Prior to Any Possible Treatment of Psychosis"? Entailed by the structure of the metaphor as well as the accompanying constructions, I have affirmed it for a long time. In following them, one could put the Name-of-the-Father in the place of the quilting point [*point de capiton*] for the entirety of the chain of discourse, including the chain of the unconscious and the phallic signifier that is subordinated to the one of the Father, as a key for the whole of the signified.

This was Lacan's starting point. The quilting point supposes a signifier that stops the drift of the signification, as in the simplest sentence where the signification remains in suspense until the very last word. We recall the famous development of Lacan about the first scene of *Athalie* by Jean Racine, but it is true for any sentence.

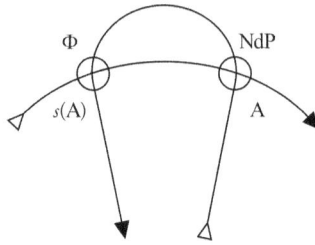

Figure 6.1 The Name-of-the-Father as quilting point

For example: "That one says . . ." ["*Qu'on dise . . .*"], interruption of the significa-tion, "That one says remains", another interruption, "That one says remains forgot-ten", first quilting point; at this point, one signification is posed although it is not yet the end of the sentence. To speak of the signifying chain, unconscious or not, supposes a signifier that fixes the end of the chain and puts a halt to the signifying effect with a first signification, which can then be interrogated as to its meaning. This construction implied placing the Name-of-the-Father in the Other as signifier of its Law. This is what Lacan explicitly did, and this is how he formulates it in "On a Question Prior to Any Possible Treatment of Psychosis", making it what holds the entire symbolic system together.

We know the point of arrival of his trajectory, he turns things around, and I have highlighted it. The unconscious is not a signifying chain; it is not the signifying chain of the subject; it ciphers its jouissance, and the unconscious is real. It is an ef-fect of *lalangue* on the body, it is a "speaking-being" [*parlêtre*], it does not suppose the quilting point that the discourse of the subject implies, and the jouissance that is produced is . . . phallic. Yet there are different turning points in the conception with their respective reasons. On this matter, one turning point is taken in "The Subversion of the Subject and the Dialectic of Desire", therefore at the time Lacan delivers his graph, and this is maybe why he held it back for so long, well before the seminar *Encore* that is generally considered to be itself a turning point.

I will start again with the well-known thesis in "On a Question Prior to Any Pos-sible Treatment of Psychosis" and the function of the paternal metaphor. As in every metaphor, the signifier that is substituted for the one that is repressed produces in it a (+) at the level of the signified, a (+) that one may qualify as imaginary, as per the schema of the subordination of the imaginary to the symbolic, $S/s = S/I$. Thus the metaphor, while substituting the Name-of-the-Father for the desire of the Mother, elicits a plus in the imaginary of the signified, the famous phallic signification. The signifier DM, the desire of the Mother, a desire that is symbolised by her absence, already writes one signification of lack but a lack that is undetermined and that Lacan first wrote with an x. It is the x of the "Che vuoi?" The metaphor gives it its signifier, the phallus. This (the phallus) is what the plus is at the level of the signified. And it is categorical; it is "a signification that is evoked only by what I call a metaphor – to be precise, the paternal metaphor" (Lacan, [1959] 2006, p. 463). I would like to emphasise the "only", the logical conclusion being that the P_0 of the foreclosure in the symbolic implied for the subject the φ_0 in the Imaginary of the signification.[1]

Note

1 P_0 is the lack of the Name-of-the-Father and φ_0 is the lack of the (imaginary) castrated phallus. See the I-Schema (Lacan, [1959] 2006, p. 467).

References

Lacan, J. (2001 [1973]). Introduction à l'édition allemande d'un premier volume des Écrits. In: *Autres écrits* (pp. 553–559). Paris: Éditions du Seuil.

Lacan, J. (2006 [1959]). On a Question Prior to Any Possible Treatment of Psychosis. In: *Écrits: The First Complete Edition in English*. B. Fink (Trans.). New York: Norton.

Lacan, J. (2006 [1961]). The Direction of the Treatment and the Principles of Its Power. In: *Écrits: The First Complete Edition in English*. B. Fink (Trans.). New York: Norton.

Lacan, J. (2006 [1966a]). The Signification of the Phallus. In: *Écrits: The First Complete Edition in English*. B. Fink (Trans.). New York: Norton.

Lacan, J. (2006 [1966b]). The Subversion of the Subject and the Dialectic of Desire in the Freudian Unconscious. In: *Écrits: The First Complete Edition in English*. B. Fink (Trans.). New York: Norton.

Soler, C. (2006). *What Lacan Said About Women: A Psychoanalytic Study*. J. Holland (Trans.). New York: Other Press.

Chapter 7

11th March 2015

I remind you where I stopped last time. I demonstrated that the imaginary and symbolic identifications with the semblable and with the Other are determined by desire and thus pass through the mediation of the phallic signifier. Hence the importance of knowing if this signifier is subordinated or not to that of the Father, as it was posited in "On a Question Prior to Any Possible Treatment of Psychosis". From there, I will return to the first thesis, namely that phallic signification is evoked *only* through metaphor. I have highlighted the ambiguity of this signification which evokes both lack in being and lack in enjoying and which, on the other hand, only takes its efficacy from being perceived in the Other, that is, the Mother, as is generally said.

The primordial identification

In constructing his R schema, which he called that of "the subjective constitution" and which, according to him, conditions the very perception of reality that psychosis disturbs, Lacan situates the phallus at the foundation of a primordial identification which is different from what he says about it concerning the butcher's wife or, more generally speaking, about the neurotic.

Indeed, he is not talking about the signifier but about the "phallic image", where – I quote – "the subject identifies . . . with its living being". What is the living being of a subject [*l'être de vivant d'un sujet*]? This subject is not written S in the R schema; it is written S to designate what he calls "its reality, foreclosed as such in the system". That is, the symbolic system, that of the Other, where it is certainly inscribed, but under the signifiers of the Other because it is spoken of even before being born in the anticipation of what is expected from it and in perfect misrecognition of the singular characteristics that will be its own. "Let it turn out to be a hermaphrodite and see what happens!" Lacan says somewhere. In the beginning, it thus enters into the play of signifiers only in the form of the dummy [*mort*], basically as a pure supposed [*supposé*]. But Lacan adds: "it is as a living being" that it will play its part. I remind you that the life of the subject is not that of the organism; it is not animal vitality, which is precisely what the infant loses as he enters language and succumbs to its mortification. Lacan has a beautiful expression

DOI: 10.4324/9781032645506-7

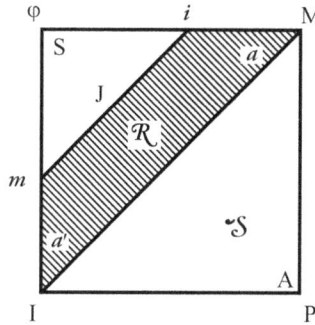

Figure 7.1 R Schema
Source: Lacan (1959 [2006], p. 462)

to describe this hiatus between the natural subject, S, and the subject effect of the signifier, $. He evokes the "ineffable and stupid existence", in other words, the without-reason [*le sans raison*] for its being in the world. Here, we already have an indication of the dimension of a real outside the symbolic, the one that will be written in the Borromean knot as an autonomous dimension in regard to the symbolic. This is why it is traversed by "the question of its existence" and must identify with its living being [*etre de vivant*]. His thesis is that the Other's desire is necessary because, insofar as it is a desired child in the Other, it is already identified with the signifier of the phallus, which thus allows it to knot the without-reason of its real existence to the symbolic. But when it comes to its own life, I have emphasised previously, the subject appears as living only when it makes "its entry into the real", thus when it subtracts itself from the Other – the term is Lacan's – when therefore, by means of the articulation of demand, it is born as a libidinal subject, gifted with the life of desire of which Lacan says it is "borne by death", that is to say, by the negativising effect of language. The phallus gives its signifier to this life of the subject which is desire.

It is from this hole in the Imaginary, caused by the failure of identification with the phallus in the case of foreclosure, that Lacan attempted to think of a whole series of phenomena proper to psychosis. First and foremost with regard to what Schreber calls "soul-murder", he diagnoses a disorder, I quote, "at the inmost juncture of the subject's sense of life" (Lacan, [1959] 2006, p. 466). What does this disturbance of the sense of life mean clinically? We know the two extreme forms of it: the pain of existence when it leads to melancholia, and in contrast, the pathological manic vitality, or even the alternating of the two, whereas the subject's sense of life, as a general rule, is strictly correlated to desire. Another phenomenon concerns the identifications. The latter are not lacking in psychosis. For Schreber himself, Lacan postulates "the identification, whatever it may be, by which the subject assumed [*a assumé*] his mother's desire" (Ibid, p. 472) right up until the triggering [*déclenchement*]. What characterises them? Clinically, we observe it, as far as the imaginary identifications with the semblable are concerned, they sometimes go as far as transitivism; and as far as identifications with the Other are concerned, even right up to the quasi-debile "as if". These are "immediate" identifications, as Lacan said in the beginning. The term does not refer to their temporality, but rather to the absence of mediation. I explained how the identifications mentioned on the graph generally passed through the mediation of the phallus that they veil and which is thus maintained in repression. Jean-Jacques Rousseau has described wonderful instances of these identifications in which the subject does not feign anything, as he says, but becomes another.

In any case, with this primordial identification, we see that the phallus, which is the signifier of the desire of/for the Mother, also becomes the signifier of the subject's being, which, therefore, finds itself from the start connected to the Other. It makes of the subject a social being at origin and thus gives to the metaphor a socialising function dependent on the Father function. Hence, we understand that the question of what conditions this primordial identification with the signifier of the lack in the Other is crucial. Furthermore, we can also question the metaphor regarding a possible sexualising function. It has been said, I have said it myself, that as soon as the phallus comes to specify the DM, the desire of the Mother, this metaphor ensured the entry onto the scene of the woman's sexual desire. This can be discussed, and I will come back to it when I speak about the role of identifications in sexuality.

Subversion

Let me now come back to the turning point that calls into question the construction of the paternal metaphor in "The Subversion of the Subject and the Dialectic of Desire in the Freudian Unconscious". This is what I will examine now.

From "On a Question Prior" right up to "Subversion of the Subject and the Dialectic of Desire", Lacan developed and specified the very notion of the phallus, its definition, its function, its writing, presupposing, or at least suggesting without ever coming back to it, its subordination to the signifier of the Father introduced with the paternal metaphor. The writing S(Ⱥ) and the formula that he will constantly repeat from that moment on, "There is no Other of the Other", suffice to demolish this construction. But where does this rectification proceed from? From logic itself, not just any logic, not Aristotle's logic but the logic of set theory. Later on, his use of the logic of sets, his references to Russell, Gödel and Frege will be more systematic and explicit; but starting from this text, Lacan evokes the paradoxes of logic (Lacan, [1966b] 2006, p. 693). S(Ⱥ) writes the logical inconsistency of the Other as the locus of signifiers. It is, I quote: "symbolised by the inherence of a (−1) in the set of signifiers" (Ibid, p. 694). He further says that it is "a line that traces itself from its circle", the circle of the treasure trove of signifiers. It is an implicit reference to both Russell's paradox of the catalogue of catalogues and Gödel's theorem: a set requires a term outside the set, thus a (−1). Lacan explicitly posed the Name-of-the-Father as a (+1), which, in the Other, is the signifier of its law.

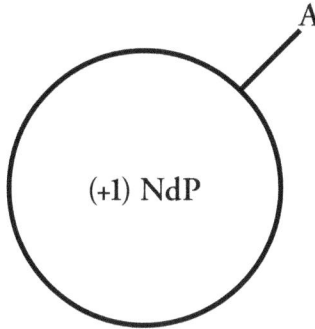

Figure 7.2 The Name-of-the-Father as the law of the Other

And this is what he amends.

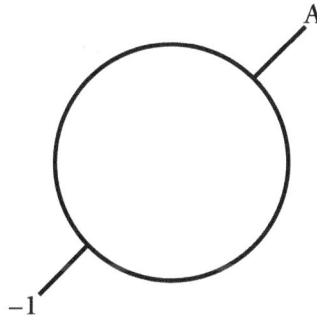

Figure 7.3 S(Ⱥ) as the inconsistency of the Other

In the graph, in the place where the signification of the unconscious chain is button tied [*se capitonne*], he writes S(Ⱥ), which is symbolised by (−1), and he specifies that it is "the privileged place of jouissance", this jouissance which, lacking in the Other, makes it inconsistent, Ⱥ. And this is the very same place that Φ (capital phi), signifier of "the jouissance that cannot be negativised", comes to occupy. So here is what fastens [*boucle*] the signification of the unconscious chain; it is explicit. Hence, with the graph, no Name-of-the-Father within the Other, end of the metaphor, but that end does not jeopardise the button-tying [*capitonnage*] of the unconscious chain, which is, since Freud, the repressed chain of jouissance. Therefore, we see that this chain of jouissance is written between two terms: the treasury of drives on the one hand and the capital Φ on the other. Jouissance can only be written as drive jouissance or as phallic jouissance, and this without the Father. We have there, already, the foundation of what will lead us to the "no sexual relation" in later years. The autonomy of the phallic function in relation to the Father is surely implied there; that is why I have insisted on the fact that the phallic signifier was placed in the graph on all the levels as the signifier of the effects of the signifier on the signified, as $-\varphi$ in the fantasy – Lacan developed it at length – and as Φ in the place of jouissance. However, as often happened, Lacan himself did not underline this shift, and consequently, we continue to maintain the thesis of the subordination of the phallic function to the Father. Fortunately, he made it explicit in *Le sinthome* which allows us to read it retroactively as early as "Subversion of the Subject".

The function of S($\mathcal{A}$), on the other hand, Lacan clarifies. Provided that the signifier represents a subject for other signifiers, it is written thus: $S_1 \longrightarrow S_2$. S($\mathcal{A}$) is, I quote, "the signifier to which all the other signifiers represent the subject – which means that if this signifier is missing, all the other signifiers represent nothing." (Ibid.). We need to write then:

$$\frac{S_1}{\mathcal{S}} \longrightarrow S\ (\mathcal{A})$$

The subject is represented to (*auprès*) the signifier of the jouissance or the signifier that marks the place of the jouissance.

When Lacan writes later on, notably in *Encore*, that the subject is represented to (*auprès*) unconscious knowledge, to signifiers of *lalangue* that mark the body and that preside over jouissance, it is a development of this writing in which unconscious knowledge has come to the place of S($\mathcal{A}$).

I hope you now have a sense of the extent to which "Subversion of the Subject" is a moment of subversion at the very heart of Lacan's teaching. It implies a new contribution with regard to the quilting point [*point de capiton*]. The latter is inherent to the notion of the signifying chain, and from the beginning, it was thought of as produced by a signifier, the one we usually write as S2. But with this graph, we enter into another theme; it is jouissance that decides on the quilting point. That is why I wrote a text titled "The commandments of jouissance" which, moreover, had the honour of being magisterially censured in the former School. What it adds implicitly is that the signifier which quilts is either determined by jouissance, or causes it, or is itself enjoyed. Moreover, the simplest practice of speech can give us a hint of it since it often happens that we search for words, we correct ourselves. Admittedly, this is not an experience that gives the idea of jouissance, but all the same, it suggests that there is a principle of choice, and the choice cannot come solely from the signifier. If there is a choice of signifier, this choice can only come from a being that has an aim [*une visée*].

Copulatory function of the phallus

I return to the phallic dialectic, which, as I have shown, Lacan had freed from its dependence on the signifier of the Father, to find out what is the measure of its clinical significance, specifically on the sexual level, since it is on this level that there is a problem. We can only be struck by the equivocity of this term, *phallus*: signifier of the lack of castration [*signifiant du manque de la castration*], but also the signifier of power, particularly, but not exclusively, sexual. Starting from "The Signification of the Phallus", these two sides of the signifier were posed. It is the signifier of the power that the signifier has on the signifiable, which it transforms into signified. As a result, it is also the signifier of the division, *Spaltung* of the subject which results from the signifying effect, the subject which "in any case . . . cannot aim at being whole" (Lacan, [1966a] 2006, p. 581). Therefore, when we say the power of the signifier, this means castration of the subject, and, I quote, the "Logos is wedded to the advent of desire" (Ibid.). In this genealogy of desire, starting from the logos, sex – along with what it involves in terms of bodies and in terms of the *sex-ratio* of the male/female difference, which is real, not linguistic – sex does not have a place, but the phallus makes up for it.

We know how Lacan has accentuated, as distinct from Freud, the opposition not between having or not having the penis but between having or being the phallus. I will pause on what is meant by the expressions to have or not have the phallus; it is crucial for situating the so-called maternal castration and the concept of castration itself. Lacan's thesis is explicit. The phallic signifier, on the level of castration strictly speaking – to be distinguished from frustration and privation – functions as an object. An imaginary object in the relation between the subject and its partners. On this point, it seems Freud made too much of the simple absence of the penis since this absence did not prevent the proliferation of analytic discussions regarding the non-castrated Mother, the Mother said to be phallic, even castrating. Clinically we observe that the absence of a penis, which fundamentally is real, takes up function in the child's subjectivity only when it takes on the value of absence of the phallus, insignia of what is desirable, of the desirable which, in its distinction from need, is an effect of the signifier. The absence of the penis has the value of absence of the phallus only if what is inscribed "in the subject's unconscious is the Other's desire [*le désir de l'Autre*], that is, [a desire for] the phallus that was desired by the Mother." (Lacan, [1962] 2006, p. 617). Everything begins then with what is the phallicisation of the desirable. The phallus makes a copula between the subject and the Other; it has a mediating function between the subjectivities of the subject and of the Other. But it summons them no less when it comes to the conjunction between bodies and when it comes to articulating the difference between masculine and feminine desire. Both are desire of the phallus as desire of the Other, but one, the woman, finds the "signifier of her own desire in the body of the person to whom her demand for love is addressed." (Lacan, [1966a] 2006, p. 583). The other, the man, finds the signifier in the feminine object itself in as much as this object, a woman, does not have it. The phallus can, therefore, connect bodies that are altogether different from subjectivities, see the masculine case of the "Direction of the Treatment", and the analysis that Lacan made of the couple Alcibiades/Socrates, Socrates who does as well as the woman behind her veil.

But then, where does it come from, this original attribution of phallic lack to the Mother? Does it come from the Father of the metaphor, as we used to believe? But why, then, does Lacan end the *Écrits* on the Mother's lack of the penis, based on which he distributes the relation to castration in the diverse clinical structures, as if it were simply from that, from this lack of penis, that the phallicism of sexual desire might originate?

Lacan well perceived that between being and having a small articulation was necessary. In "On a Question Prior", he said that if "being and having are mutually exclusive in theory, they overlap, at least as far as the result is concerned, when a lack is at stake." (Lacan, [1959] 2006, p. 471). Strange: to have a lack and to be a lack is, therefore, one and the same thing. We could have thought, on the contrary, that on the sexual level, there where the body is therefore engaged, the phallus is the signifier of the castration of one, the woman, and of the power of the Other, the man. That would have been a return to the Freudian idea simply transposed in terms of the signifier. But there we encounter the difference between Lacan's formulas and their apparent paradox: for him, castration is on the side of the one who has the organ, and it is what founds his desire, the desire which Lacan made proper to the man, not to the woman, and thus he lays claim to Freud's strange thesis of one sole libido, the masculine, and it goes for all subjects, even when it lodges in a woman.

You see from "Guiding Remarks for a Convention on Female Sexuality", it is very clear: "the desire that castration liberates in the male in giving him the phallus as its signifier" (Lacan, [1962] 2006, p. 619) and he calls men "desire's supporters" (Ibid.) ["*les tenants du désir*"]. Hence, the idea that desiring is not feminine; desiring is to play the part of the man [*faire l'homme*]. Women, by contrast, he calls "the appellants of sex" [*les appelants du sexe*], demanding both love and the organ. It is a great constant in Lacan's teaching, which is found again in "L'étourdit": "there is no virility that castration does not consecrate" (Ibid., p. 617), whence the idea that what feminine desire appeals to, wishes for, beyond the veil, is the "castrated lover", whereas being the phallus, being desired, feminises. And later, he proposes more complex formulas: "The man is not without having it" since it is on this side that a woman seeks it, sexually speaking, and mirroring this, "the woman is not without being it" given that the desire of a man situates her as the object which he lacks. One could say then that one, the woman, signifies to the other, "you have the object of my lack", while the other, the man, "you are the object of my lack". But that would be a mistake; it is not symmetrical since she only stands in for the phallus, whereas the organ, "the attribute which she cherishes", is not a placeholder. I will return to the measure of this efficacy of the phallic copula.

References

Lacan, J. (2006 [1959]). On a Question Prior to Any Possible Treatment of Psychosis. In: *Écrits: The First Complete Edition in English*. B. Fink (Trans.). New York: Norton.

Lacan, J. (2006 [1962]). Guiding Remarks for a Convention on Female Sexuality. In: *Écrits: The First Complete Edition in English*. B. Fink (Trans.). New York: Norton.

Lacan, J. (2006 [1966a]). The Signification of the Phallus. In: *Écrits: The First Complete Edition in English*. B. Fink (Trans.). New York: Norton.

Lacan, J. (2006 [1966b]). The Subversion of the Subject and the Dialectic of Desire in the Freudian Unconscious. In: *Écrits: The First Complete Edition in English*. B. Fink (Trans.). New York: Norton.

Chapter 8

25th March 2015

I continue on the efficacy of the phallic function. I recalled what is the secret of the subject's constitutive identifications in accordance with the graph, and also the copula of the play between the sexes. In every case, for Freud as for Lacan, in the texts to which I have referred, it depends upon [*suspendue*] castration, the so-called maternal one.

Maternal castration

But I am stopping for a moment at the point where I left things in suspense: the crucial question of what conditions the emergence, starting from the mother's lack of a penis, of the phallic signification of maternal desire, a signification from which everything begins according to Freud and Lacan.

The metaphor made us think that for phallic signification to emerge, the Name-of-the-Father was necessary. I have shown that the autonomy of this phallic dimension is postulated by the graph, so-called of desire. It nevertheless remains that the signifier of the Father could be the operator, not of the presence of the phallic signifier, but of the emergence of this crucial signification which is the signification of maternal castration. In this regard, I see a major ambiguity in the paternal metaphor. Ordering the two signifiers of generation, father/mother, and the two signifiers of the reproductive couple, man and woman, it can be taken as a version of the Oedipus of families. Indeed, one could think that, with the substitution of the signifier man-father for that of the mother, the desire of the mother thus takes on a sexual signification. This is not how Lacan understood it, since in his writing of the metaphor, in the effect produced, the mother no longer figures, but instead the Other with a capital O. And yet this is how it has been read. Except that this sexualisation or rather this phallicisation of the desire of the mother by the metaphor presupposes making the father homologous with the role of the hetero-man, that is, the genitor. But Lacan insisted, from the beginning to the end, and he reaffirms it in *Télévision*: the father of the metaphor is not the genitor, not even necessarily present in the family. It is a pure signifier, hence the notion of "dead father"; more parent to the Logos than of the flesh. Thus, how could it sexualise anything?

DOI: 10.4324/9781032645506-8

I think Lacan grasped the problem, and I found confirmation for it in the following fact. The year after *The Psychoses*, Lacan proceeded to the seminar *The Object Relation*, at the time an established notion, and he commented on Freud's case of Little Hans. Currently, in our community, we make much of this and draw from it an argument about the sexualising function of the father. But what does the text show? Lacan begins by highlighting the complicit game of seduction between the child and the mother. Thus the phallus is there before the phobia, covered over by the demand for love: to be what the Other lacks. The phobia does not appear until later to respond to the newly emerged question of sex and, correlatively, the question of knowing what it is to be a man. Those questions and this phobia are introduced through the conjunction of two givens: on the one hand, the erogenous activity of the organ – which poses the problem of its function between the subject and the Other beyond the seduction game – and on the other hand, by the sexual discord of the parents; the father does not fuck the mother, the organ can hardly take on a sexual meaning. Thus it is not at all the Name-of-the-Father, which is not missing, that introduces the problematics of sex; it is the jouissance of the organ in need of phallic signification. That is to say, in order to sexualise, to make of the desire of the Other, the Mother, a woman's desire, something other than the metaphor is needed. And it is clear that in his analysis of Hans, Lacan is looking for this other on the side of the body and from the parents in their function as a model sexual couple. Daddy and mummy as man and woman in the same bed, which makes the daddy something altogether different from the dead father of the signifier of the metaphor. Lacan even speaks of the real father.

Parenthesis: I note nevertheless that, in saying "Name-of-the-Father", Lacan was already speaking of something other than the signifier of the Father for, strictly speaking, a name is not a signifier; a name is always an index of a real. This specificity of the name, Lacan stated in other terms, starting from "The Subversion of the Subject and the Dialectic of Desire", in his commentary on the minus-One of $S(\bar{A})$. He says it is an unpronounceable signifier but whose operation is present each time a proper name is pronounced. And he thus defines the proper name: its enunciation equals its signification. This means that the name is never equivocal, as opposed to the signifier, which always refers to other signifiers, whose enunciation, for this reason, is never equal to its signification. We could have applied to the proper name what he later applied to the letter of the symptom: identical to itself. And that places the proper name outside the field of the Other in the same way as $S(\bar{A})$. But a name does not lend itself to metaphor, and therefore, Lacan says: signifier of the Name-of-the-Father.

I come back to the phallic function in order to question the limits of its efficacy. How far does it go? What, after all, is the scope of the phallicisation of desire starting from that of the desire of the Other? In other words, what is the scope of this couple, having and being the phallus, that Lacan made correspond to the couple Man/Woman? With this construction, he accounts for the orientation of desire towards the other sex, that is, the orientation of desire towards the compatible partner who complements the phallic lack. We know that Freud expected his "little hystory" ["*hystoriole*"] of Oedipus to ensure, through identifications issuing from Oedipal loves, the becoming a man or woman of the boy and girl, in other words, sexual conformity, as well as its vicissitudes. Thus he endowed the father with a function of sexual normalisation. Lacan and especially his readers expected, indeed still expect, the same thing from the paternal metaphor. For a long time, Lacan stated categorically: this function of the Name-of-the-Father was necessary to allow each person "the assumption of one's sex", to allow the woman, as he said elsewhere, to properly respond to the needs of the child and of the man, to allow the little boy to become a heterosexual man, and the little girl to become a woman, that is to say, a man's woman. The royal road to sexual conformity thus presupposed the function of the father; and by the way, with this function, homosexuality can only be viewed as a failure. But Lacan very quickly saw the insufficiency of this thesis, and I have shown this. Indeed, a question remained in suspense: beyond desire, does the paternal function touch the real of sex which is at once that of reproduction and, for the one who speaks [*parlant*], that of the jouissance called sexual? Lacan produced the answer. The phallus makes the copula between the subject and the Other, the Other who speaks as much as the Other's body towards which it (the subject) directs itself; but paradoxically, in the end, the so-called act of copulation is not copulatory at the level of the jouissances. This is the meaning of "no sexual relation". And starting from "Position of the Unconscious", Lacan distinguished what he called the side of the living [*vivant*], where he places the drives as the only path of access to the Other sex, and the side of the Other from which the subject constructs his foundation.

The phallic supplement

"L'étourdit" offers a complement to the formulae of sexuation. I will stop for a moment on this. "Formulae of sexuation" is not about phallicisation since the phallic function is everywhere, on both sides of the aforementioned sexualisation. With these formulae, Lacan attempted a matheme of sexual identity, which would not be a semblant, which would engage a real. Which one? We could say that of the subject, since for it, there is only one real, that of castration and, in addition, the real of jouissance which supposes the living [*le vivant*]. We can say this because the term sexuation implies something like a process or in any case, an operation, such as socialisation, privatisation, etc.; an operation, therefore, but one that is not reduced to an identification. The *all* and the *not all* do not designate identifications but rather a relation to castration. We know the aim – Lacan has stated it. He seeks to explain how, through discourse, two halves can be constructed that correspond well enough to the two halves of the natural *sex ratio* to assure the reproduction of bodies. This is the same problem Freud attempted to solve with his Oedipus; the distribution is made in relation to the phallic function as function of castration. Lacan refers again to his couple of being or having the phallus (Lacan, 1973, p. 14) developed in "Signification of the Phallus" among other places, to designate "the function which makes up for the sexual relation". What does it make up for?

In "Signification of the Phallus", this dialectic of being and having allows for the establishment of a link between man and woman at the level of the semblants, of appearance [*paraître*]. In 1972, Lacan added the consideration of jouissance, which he writes as capital phi, Φ, in "Subversion of the Subject and the Dialectic of Desire", but which is precisely the one that excludes the sexual relation, the relation between jouissances.

Once again, a beautiful construction, but it only accounts for a possible [*un possible*], given that, since they have a choice, they can be on one side or the other independent of their anatomy. Lacan makes it clear nothing assures that we will obtain two sexuated halves corresponding to the *sex ratio*, such as we obtained when the discourses "used to hold in place". I really believe this is what we are in the course of observing. We see the stages. From early on, I have insisted on this: phallicisation governed the ideals of sex – the semblants that give the airs of woman and man, always subject to historical variations – but fundamentally not the act itself. In "L'étourdit" the operation of sexuation passes through the differential distribution of phallic jouissance. This is a real.

But how far did Lacan go with "L'étourdit"? The phallic semblant, written in "L'étourdit" with a capital, Φ, is not the same as that in the dialectic of having and being, which determined the desire at stake in the pantomime of sexual ideals but not their real jouissance. He nevertheless again summons this dialectic: "There is nothing excessive in our experience that would lead us to give precedence to being or to having the phallus, (cf. my *Bedeutung* in *Écrits*), the function that makes up for [*supplée*] the sexual relation" (Ibid.). But this time, he wrote the function with a capital phi, Φx, a reference to Frege's propositional function, in order to say that it engages more than semblants: jouissance. To have or to be the Phallus written with a capital, this is to have or to be the signifier of the jouissance that is lacking to the partner, not only to have or to be the lack in being of the Other. And he uses the expression "supplement" to designate this function. Supplement, is a term that we use for psychosis when we ask what makes up for [*supplée*] the foreclosed Name-of-the-Father. Here the phallus makes up for the sexual relation foreclosed by language, which can be neither enunciated nor written. It makes up for it because it permits the establishment of a link to the Other sex and also a compensatory [*supplétive*] jouissance, the phallic jouissance. Regarding this jouissance, we can, of course, say, as he did in *Encore*, "that's not it" [*ça n'est pas ça*] but even so, in the absence of a jouissance that would make a relation, it *is*. It is a jouissance which thus supplements but also creates an obstacle to the man enjoying . . . the woman. This is what Lacan clarifies in *Télévision*, thus after "L'étourdit". The airs of sex, which have a function in love and in the link, are forfeited in the moment of truth of the act. I quote: "But that is why truth is more often than not standoffish, demanding of love sexual pretenses that it can't fulfill, misfiring-sure as clockwork" (Lacan, [1974] 1990, p. 41).

Let us take a look then at what, finally, this phallic supplement promises. It permits the dividing up of those who speak [*les parlants*] into the alternative of *all* or *not all* of phallic jouissance, but a first, important reservation, if we believe Lacan, this alternative is not binding. That subjects have a choice suffices to ensure that the *sex ratio* is not assured; I mean that it is not assured that human beings continue to divide themselves into two halves homologous to those of their anatomical sex. I believe we are confirming this at the beginning of this century, and we see here the extent to which Lacan had his finger on the pulse of the times.

Second reservation, this function accounts for neither the choice of the type of partner nor for the conditions of the *jouissance* obtained from it. Thus it is obvious that, in the *all phallic*, Lacan makes it clear, there are heteros, homos, and also abstentionists. Identification with one side or the other does not determine the type of couple that will suit the subject, thus leaving in suspense the question of knowing how this is determined. I am not going to go into this question; I am only indicating the answers Lacan has given. He first answered with the thesis of the partner-object, which means that it is not standard but rather determined by the fantasy proper to each subject. The "no sexual relation" conjugated with the relations which certainly occur between the sexuated implies that the partner is . . . a chance encounter [*de rencontre*]. These are the ABCs of experience, both inside and outside analysis. How does a man find a woman? Lacan jokingly replies: by chance, [*Tuchè*]; love falls under the regime of the encounter, that is, of the modality of contingency. In the encounter, which the structure imposes as necessary owing to the non-inscription of the relation, the subject repeats itself; it repeats itself as a One without the Other, missed encounter, but an encounter of the One with the *a* of its fantasy. This is what *Télévision* posits: "The subject is happy-go-lucky [*heureux*]. It is his very definition, since he can owe nothing if not to luck, to fortune in other words, and any piece of luck is good as something to maintain him, insofar as it repeats itself" (Ibid., p. 22). It repeats itself as One all alone.

The thesis will lead to the "*y a de l'Un*"[1] even in the relation. This was the first part of the thesis. It does not say where the jouissance that is obtained from this partner comes from. "L'étourdit" answers: "Nothing operates therefore except from signifying equivocation, or from the trick by which the *ab-sens* of the relationship might be plugged" (Lacan, 1973 [2001], p. 459), and this will lead Lacan to say a little later, you enjoy your unconscious, even in bed, and the partner is a symptom, a jouissance symptom, which complements the partner object cause of desire. Thus jouissance comes also from the unconscious, not in the sense of the chain of the fantasy, but in the sense of the real unconscious, outside meaning, which marries the word, that is, *lalangue*, and jouissance. I will not develop these very complex theses, little assimilated in practice; I only mention them to indicate the limit of what the formulae of sexuation assure when it comes to accounting for the coupling of bodies since to say partner-symptom is to say that the "y a de l'Un" is realised in the very heart of the couple of jouissance.

The collective and the individual

I will now move on to a whole new chapter concerning the scope of identifications, as they have been thought of thus far in the analytic movement by Freud and Lacan. They operate in two distinct fields, first at the level of the constitution of what Freud calls the *Ich*, a term that equivocates between what Lacan calls, respectively, the ego and the subject. These are identifications that one can call constitutive, and everything I have recalled about the graph of desire goes in this direction. And then there are the identifications pertaining to relations between the members of a collective, which can be expressed in various terms: group, crowd, mass, society. The subject being constituted by identification is a social being, but at this level, the identifications have a specific function, let's call it social cement, an altogether different problem. The question has to do with the relationship between the two levels of the individual and the collective. Psychoanalysis is often accused of focusing only on the first.

Context

It was Freud who introduced into psychoanalysis the problem of the social link in his 1921 text *Group Psychology and the Analysis of the Ego*. What is the backdrop to his concerns? I would like to put into perspective the appearance of this new theoretical problem in Freud as well as in Lacan since we inherit it from another context and because practical-theoretical questions never appear out of nowhere.

Freud opens his text with a summary of theses from Le Bon, who himself made use of prior theses, I quote, "repeated in unison by thinkers, statesmen and writers since the earliest periods of literature" (Freud, [1921] 1955, p. 82). Thus, a prior consensus regarding the critique, the denunciation of group effects on the individual, which, it must be said, extend to us. Freud does not dispute this; he designates what he calls "the two axioms of group psychology" namely "the intensification of the affects and the inhibition of the intellect" (Ibid.).[2] Axiom implies that this is something we take for granted. You see the presuppositions of the axiom: it assumes an idea of the individual in whom thought would not be inhibited, and affects not intensified. This is the idea of an individual from the time of the Enlightenment, unthinkable before the eighteenth century. The crowd is critiqued in the name of the individual taken as a value, defined by his rationality. Besides, Freud speaks of the "advance from group psychology to individual psychology" (Ibid., 135). But what is the historical context? He wrote in 1921, the Russian Revolution had taken place, and we know the extent to which Freud did not support the mounting collectivism of the communist ideal. As for Nazism, certainly, it had not yet triumphed but was rising; this is why Lacan can say that this text was premonitory. No doubt, on the horizon of his text, was the perceived risk of the rising collectivisms that led to the drama of the twentieth century.

But, at the same time, the consequences of the great catastrophe of the 1914 war actualised another risk, causing a passing to the act of a formidable power of unlinking. Indeed, this war marked a turning point because it touches the joint which connects individuals to the group. Durkheim (1858–1917), a sociologist, attempted to clarify, in a very convincing way, what constitutes the social feeling of belonging, what today is called integration. It has to do, according to Durkheim, with two expectations: the protection afforded by belonging to a collective of whatever kind, and the recognition that an individual can find there. Protection and recognition were therefore considered to be what would make an individual identify with a social group. However, this war and the economic disaster it caused shook these to the core (cf. the war neuroses that Freud evokes in his text) and doubtless began to affect the link between the individual and group affiliation. Moreover, it was perhaps their undermining that made perceptible the link described by Durkheim.

But in addition and at the same time, the text is situated in the wake of Freud's own advance in *Beyond the Pleasure Principle* and the death drive – which, according to Lacan, designates the register of jouissance. There, the perceived risk is quite different. It is not that of blind crowds but the reverse, that of unlinking, of the rupture of libidinal links, which are vital links for individuals. In Freud, this perceived risk is not fantasmatic, as it often is today among certain contemporaries. He discovered the power of unlinking in the transference, which he named death drive, through the construction of his concept of repetition.

This coincidence between what is elaborated in the analytic experience, always individual, and the historical events of the social body is a solid indication in favor of what Freud affirms, namely, that the two fields, although not identical, are not heterogeneous but ordered by the same forces that have constituted the individual.

Let's take a look at Lacan. He wrote the structure of his discourses as social links two years after the events of May 1968. The student protest was only one of its aspects, but it called into question the hierarchical links in the university, the family, politics, in other words, the prohibitions and norms of the time, let's say the S_1's in operation. Indeed, in the multiple voices of the protesters, there were two poles: the anarchist, humorous "it is forbidden to forbid" tendency, but also the collectivising tendency of the Little Red Book and its cultural revolution – one would do better to call it cultural repression – which was the loudest and which hilariously contested the master in the name of Mao! Lacan delivered an interpretation to the hecklers: "What you, as revolutionaries, aspire to is a master" (Lacan, [1974] 1990, p. 32), clearly targeting the second tendency, the one that concerned him directly in his family. In any case, in 1968, an order seemed threatened, the established order, and the outcome remained in suspense, still uncertain. Nevertheless, he began his seminar on the discourses in the autumn of 1969, and, let us note, his intention was not to defend the past as some did and continue to do. His elaboration, like Freud's, responded to a risk that was looming, at least from a certain side, namely: the temptation of totalitarianism. In France, it did not take on the terrorist form it had in Germany with the Baader-Meinhof Gang and in Italy with the Red Brigades, but it was there, and Lacan's position is not in doubt. See the middle of p. 30 of *Télévision*. He absolves family repression of the curse on sex and gives it credit for leaving in place what the established order in the East, in the two Communist blocks excludes, namely "liberty even in its sketchiest form" (Ibid., p. 30). It is in this context that Lacan produced his four discourses. These are four types of social order, and there is no doubt that, as for Freud, his question is certainly theoretical, it questions the structure of possible social links and their individual effects, but in the context of a specific historical risk.

Thus I emphasise the homology with Freud. For both Freud in 1921 and Lacan in 1968, the fundamental backdrop to their elaborations was, while somewhat different, the emergence, the risk of the collectivist temptation, thus the horizon of the crowd, at a moment when the disruptive forces manifested themselves in war or revolt. But the homology goes even further. For Lacan, as for Freud, their elaborations were prompted by what they developed from the analytic experience and not from sociological or historical observation. And what would this be if not the status of jouissance beyond the pleasure principle, which, moreover, does not make a sexual relation and which imposes itself as what I have called a power of unlinking? Let us not forget that it was in "Radiophonie", in June 1970, at the very end of the seminar *The Other Side of Psychoanalysis*, that Lacan introduced the formula "there is no sexual relation" [*"il n'y a pas de rapport sexuel"*]. Thus both texts approach what Freud called collective psychology – the social sciences had not yet reached their full development – on the basis of the "subject of the individual" as the analytic experience illuminates it. Lacan also formulated it by saying that it is not from observing people's behaviour – a little kick aimed at sociology – that the death drive is invented, that is to say, this power which undoes what Eros unites.

Notes

1 Can be translated as "there is Oneness" or "there is something of the One".
2 *Ibid.* p. 88. In Strachey's translation, the phrase is "two theses", whereas "axioms" preserves the notion of a statement so well-established as to be accepted without controversy.

References

Freud, S. (1955 [1921]). Group Psychology and the Analysis of the Ego. In: *The Standard Edition of the Complete Psychological Works of Sigmund Freud, Volume XVIII (1920–1922): Beyond the Pleasure Principle, Group Psychology and Other Works* (pp. 65–144). J. Strachey (Trans.). London: Hogarth Press.

Lacan, J. (1990 [1974]). *Television: A Challenge to the Psychoanalytic Establishment.* J. Copjec (Ed.). D. Hollier, R. Krauss, A. Michelson and J. Mehlman (Trans.). New York: Norton.

Lacan, J. (2001 [1973]). L'étourdit. In: *Autres écrits* (pp. 449–498). Paris: Éditions du Seuil.

Chapter 9

8th April 2015

So, I have started a new chapter, which will lead me to the possibly collectivising function of identifications. I tried to show how for Lacan, as well as for Freud, the question of the link is introduced at the point where the historical dangers of their times converge with their strictly analytical elaborations. For Freud, it was, on the one hand, the shock produced by the War of 1914–1918 and the rise of collectivisms which were to flare up in the twentieth century, and, on the other hand, his discovery of the beyond the pleasure principle, and his death drive. For Lacan, on the one hand, the upheaval of 1968 with its collectivist temptations, however quickly aborted, and on the other hand, his elaboration of the status of non-linking *jouissances,* which reveal themselves in the analysis of symptoms.

Our context

We admittedly approach the issue in a different context, so what has changed for us today, some fifty years after Lacan? Well, the change does not come from psychoanalysis because, on this theme, no new consistent advances were produced. Freud's analyses of the structure of the crowd seem definitive and continue to instruct us. The same may be said of the advances made by Lacan on the structure of discourses that make up for the *non-rapport* and on the hiatus between, on the one hand, the real of *jouissance* – the *Y a de l'Un* over which it presides – and on the other hand, the truth of libidinal links which attach a subject to the Other and to others. These continue to guide us and, moreover, require us to elaborate, case by case, the clinic of the knot between truth and real.

By contrast, the historical context of social links has changed. Not easy to say exactly how; we nowadays note their fragmentation, thus a movement of unlinking. Lacan, at the end of his "Proposition", called it a reshaping [*remaniement*]. We are talking here about the crisis, even the end of organisations based on a symbolic hierarchy, such as the family of yesteryear. But one thing is sure and provides an indication: in the common discourse, the dominant complaint, heard in literature and through the various media, is reversed. One complained about the shackles of social constraints. One could say, "Families, I hate you" – a remark attributed to André Gide, who died in 1951 – one could shout "down with the masters". Today

DOI: 10.4324/9781032645506-9

we deplore the opposite: instability, more generally, the precariousness of links, their disintegration, the threat of isolation and rejection, all phenomena attributed to the instrumentalisation of individuals by the market, and then we shout against the impotence of State policies to protect the individual. Thus we witness the rise of defenders of a bygone world. At the last seminar of the *Champ lacanien*, two of them were evoked, Marcel Gauchet and Giorgio Agamben, who, whatever the quality of their analyses, nevertheless dream of times past: respectively that of the One (capital O) supposed to cause cohesion, and that of subjects not yet "desubjectivised." In psychoanalysis itself, this concern assumes the form of regret, nostalgia for the time when the Father was written with a capital letter, and we fear new technologies, networks, etc., ultimately, the future in the making. The future is, obviously, always disquieting because we do not know what it will give birth to, and after the twentieth century, we are no longer sure that it promises a better tomorrow. There have always been nostalgics who denounced modern times, but keep in mind that those who achieved a place in history as contemporaneous with their time are those who produced something new and who generally were not well received by their contemporaries. Think of the early twentieth century and what happened in painting, arts, literature, and . . . the birth of psychoanalysis. I insist because, in this context, analysts are summoned to take a stand, as Freud and Lacan did. To take a stand means not simply repeating what the media says – exclusion, precariousness, solitude – but above all, orienting oneself, if possible without ideology, on the basis of the analytic experience and the experience of the symptom(s).

In the footsteps of Freud

I return to Freud. I reread *Group Psychology and the Analysis of the Ego*, following the text step by step, as I sometimes do for Lacan, trying to learn not only from the enunciations but also from the steps taken. And I would like to emphasise an aspect that is not usually stressed enough. It is worth reading again the introduction to this text, the title of which clearly indicates the two fields in which identifications operate. One can perceive that Freud posed the problem of what we call today the social link, about which we worry so much, and we need to see precisely why Freud posed this problem. Moreover, he started from a prior hypothesis on the relationship between the individual and the collective.

A single psychology

I remind you of some of his words at the beginning of the introduction:

> In the individual's mental life someone else is invariably involved, as a model, as an object, as a helper, as an opponent; and so from the very first individual psychology, in this extended but entirely justifiable sense of the words, is at the same time social psychology as well.

(Freud, [1921] 1955, p. 69)

In Lacan's words, one would say the subject is a social being. On the following page, Freud specifies that in the family, the individual only comes under the influence of one or a very small number of persons with whom he is libidinally linked. The link of identifications – evoked here with the word "influence" – with the libidinal register is clearly affirmed. When Lacan, commenting on his graph, says that the subject constitutes himself in the field of the Other and that identifications, which are inscribed in his graph, "are determined by desire" (Lacan, [1964] 2006, p. 724), he is coming from the same direction, with one slight difference: he adds that those who speak [*parlants*] are determined by the signifier, by language.

Freud adds something. Individual psychology is social psychology but opposed to other processes, narcissistic, "in which the satisfaction of the instincts is partially or totally withdrawn from the influence of other people" (Freud, [1921] 1955, p. 69). There we are, already in the register of what can break the link. It is from there, from the narcissistic objection, if I may say so, that Freud approaches the problem of the crowd. He notes that in the crowd, the individual is "isolated" in the midst of numerous strangers (which means that he is not bound to them by a libidinal link), "man as a member of a race, of a nation, of a caste, of a profession, of an institution, or as a component part of a crowd of people who have been organized into a group at some particular time for some definite purpose" (Ibid., p. 70). For us who have read Lacan, all these terms, so simple, so concrete, lineage, people, etc. . . . , imply more than the number of individuals; they imply unifying *semblants*, and thus we understand that it is the question of identifications which are determined by the discourse of the master that Freud aims at addressing.

Following this reminder, this first step expressing that individual psychology is social psychology, Freud delineates the reciprocal for the group: he rejects the then fashionable idea of an original social instinct and argues that the beginnings of a supposed social instinct – which he calls in English herd instinct, group mind – are to be found in the narrower family circle, that is to say, the place where the individual libido is at play. In other words, if individual psychology is social, group psychology is itself individual. Is this not what Lacan will relay when he says, "*the collective is nothing but the subject of the individual*"? (Lacan, [1945] 2006, p. 175).

"Civilising" love

Following this, Freud firstly eliminates the theses of Le Bon and McDougall; next, he refutes suggestion – which itself needs to be explained – as the explanation for the two "axioms of the crowd", heightened affectivity and inhibited thinking. He replaces them with his own hypothesis, that of the libido, which is the energy of the sexual drives and which had already shed light on individual psychology. Freud clearly explains it and insists it is love between the sexes and love in general. He homogenises, then, what we distinguish, love as a feeling and the exigency of jouissance, and he justifies it. "Psychoanalysis, then, gives these love instincts the name of sexual instincts" (Freud, [1921] 1955, p. 91), with reference to Plato's

Eros and Saint Paul's Epistle to the Corinthians. He dots the i's and crosses the t's, love between the sexes, self-love, filial or parental love, friendship, love of mankind, of objects, of ideas; all these forms have their origin in what pushes for the union of the sexes. If we were to object based on what experience shows, namely that the aim [*la visée*] of jouissance of sexual desire is not at all identical to the love at play [*qui joue*] between the subject and the Other of speech, Freud has his answer. In love, it is the same drive but . . . inhibited in its aim. And throughout the text, we can follow his insistence on this difference between direct drives and drives inhibited in their aim – in order to grasp the use that Freud makes of it.

Freud underlines the traits that the couple and the group have in common: the tendency to get closer and . . . self-sacrifice. He thus concludes that the same drive constitutes the cement of both couples and groups. I quote: "Love relationships (or, to use a more neutral expression, emotional ties) also constitute the essence of the group mind" (Ibid.). He demonstrates it subsequently by speaking of the Church (Catholic, he specifies) and of the army. In both (and this is well known), I quote:

> The same illusion holds good of there being a head . . . who loves all the individuals in the group with an equal love. . . . There is no doubt that the tie which unites each individual with Christ is also the cause of the tie which unites them with one another.
>
> (Ibid., p. 94)

So, two links in these groups, the link of each one to the leader and the link of each to the other.

We grasp there one of the reasons for his interest in group formations. They produce what is unthinkable for Freud, that is to say, a suspension of hostile, negative feelings, of ambivalence, that is a limitation to narcissism found nowhere else except precisely in love. The group transforms the individual at the level of "what is often a profound alteration in his mental activity" (Ibid., p. 88). Outside the group, he "possessed his own continuity, his self-consciousness, his traditions and customs, his own particular functions and position, and he kept apart from his rivals" (Ibid., p. 86). One is, therefore, in the field of identity and competition. In the group, the individual loses not only his capacity to think and to judge but also renounces all his indexes of identity, even those of sex. What the social order, for us, the discourse of the master, did not manage to achieve, the group does. The hostility to the other, to the stranger, that Freud supposes to be a quasi-natural force because it is founded on the narcissistic libido, this hostility is strangely overcome to the benefit of feelings of fraternity and solidarity (at the expense of segregation).

For Freud, this is the true problem posed by the group; as I noted, it is not something we knew long before him, namely the docility of the individual in a group, with the accompanying dangers of stupidity, credulity, and the creation of what Lacan will name "party fodder" (Lacan, [1970] 2001, p. 415).[1] For Freud, at this moment, it is a question of knowing how murderous competition can be contained, and how such a limitation of the individual's combative narcissism is possible. The answer, I quote: "Such a limitation of narcissism can . . . only be produced by one factor, a libidinal tie with other people" (Freud, [1921] 1955, p. 102). Similarly, in the mythical development of humanity as a whole, "just as in individuals, love alone acts as the civilising factor" (Ibid, p. 102). Thus, in summary: from the individual to the group, one sole psychology and . . . one sole factor of cohesion, love.

But those are the drives of love, "which have been diverted from their original aims, though they do not operate with less energy on that account" (Ibid.). This is another thesis of Freud that merits our reflection: love is as strong as the sexual drive in the proper sense, so strong that it is capable of thwarting narcissism. Lacan seems to me far from this perspective, but this is because he operates with three terms and not two: love, desire and jouissance. With Lacan, the one of the graph, we could say without a doubt: desire is as strong as the aim of sexual jouissance, unlike love, and for him, it is desire, not love, that determines the identifications. However, it is more complex because there is a link between love and desire; it is that love, in as much as it is demand, conveys desire, and even when it is love that seems to operate, the secret of its force is the desire that it carries. I'll leave it there and continue with Freud, who insists a lot on the sacrificial side of love. In love, the ideal ego [*moi idéal*], which is the ego of narcissism, is impoverished to the benefit of the other, who, inflated by the transfer of libido, becomes idealised as the ego-ideal [*idéal du moi*]. Definition of love: it is thus the confusion of the object and the ideal, or a transfer of the ego-ideal [*idéal du moi*] onto the other. Freud will describe the opposition between the love that elevates the object in as much as it is inhibited in its aim and the direct sexual satisfaction that reduces it. Hence the advantage, said Freud, of drives inhibited in their aim: they are the only ones that can ensure durable links because the act establishes only the ephemeral link of the moment of possession. In our terms, love makes a link, jouissance unlinks. I will come back to that.

The three identifications

At the end of Chapter 6, we arrived at the theme of civilising love as demonstrated by the group. Then came Chapter 7: Identification. Why? Freud justifies it. After having stated his hypothesis, he makes a sidestep, asking himself if love is the only type of link to the object or if there are other linking mechanisms. He immediately affirms that, yes, there is identification, which he thus introduces as not homogenous with love but as something else, with the question of knowing how the two fit together.

About Freud's three identifications, I undertook a rereading of them with a view to specifying what he draws from them regarding the group, but they obviously interest us well beyond that, and I want to clarify how I read it. Of these three, there are two, the first and the third, that are independent of the libidinal relation to the object of love. The second distinguishes itself on this point.

I start with the first, the identification with the father, which does not pass through love; that is to say, it does not pass through object-choice and even precedes it;

Freud insists on this. One often comments on this by immediately convoking the primitive father of the horde, but we don't find any real footing there. But re-reading Freud's text, I am struck by its simplicity: "Identification is known to psychoanalysis as the earliest expression of an emotional tie with another person" (Ibid., p. 105). This link of the first identification, what is it? He takes his father as ideal, and would want to become and be like him. An exemplary identification, the characteristics of which, Freud notes, distinguish it from the choice of the father as a love object. "In the first case one's father is what one would like to *be*, and in the second he is what one would like to *have*. The distinction, that is, depends upon whether the tie attaches to the subject or to the object of the ego" (Ibid., p. 106). Thus, this link is possible before any choice of object: "identification endeavours to mould a person's own ego after the fashion of the one that has been taken as a model" (Ibid.) Note: this *being* and *having* of Freud's is a different couple than that of Lacan; it is clearly about an identification that is constitutive of the subject. So far, no problems. Freud calls it primary because it plays a role in the prehistory of the Oedipus complex. This is not "Totem and Taboo", this prehistory; it is a type of link that is independent of the difference between the sexes, of the libidinal link man/woman. Freud insists on that; independent of the Oedipal trio, it therefore does not suppose any maternal object, and even when there is a link to the mother, he says the two links remain independent. In "The Ego and the Id", he also accentuates the trait. It would be, I quote, "safer to say 'with the parents'; for before a child has arrived at definite knowledge of the difference between the sexes, the lack of a penis, it does not distinguish in value between its father and its mother" (Freud, [1923] 1961, p. 31). How can we comment on this first identification without taking into consideration what Freud writes here?

What, however, are the parents considered independent from sexual difference, if not those who incarnate the Other of Lacan? Furthermore, the essential point is if the little boy in general, that is, any little boy, regardless of the little boy he is and of the father he has, if every little boy takes his father as a model, it is certainly not because of the particular characteristics of *his own* father. Freud situates himself clearly here at the level of a universal structure, and by taking into consideration the last remark that I have cited on "the parents", he posits that every little child takes the Other, the one who, for us, is in the position of the Other, as a model. We are not so far from what Lacan aims at in his schema R. If we limit this to the father, as Freud does more often, we will say that every little boy takes his father, whoever he is, as a model. So what is the reason for that? Is it because he is bigger, stronger? This would be a recourse to the imaginary, and also, especially if we are inspired by sociology, in the family of Freud's time, every father was a social and sexual power. This would not be absurd, but it would come back to say that, in discourse, the father is a signifier of exception, as a signifier of power. To say that the father is a signifier of exception, is Freud with Lacan, which means clarified by Lacan. But to resort, as many do, to the enjoying father [*père jouisseur*] of the horde, the man of all the women, would be to conflate the Freud of 1920 with the Freud of 1913, and this would only introduce confusion because, certainly, the father of the horde is an exception, but not just any exception, one that implies a specific characteristic of jouissance, whereas Freud's paragraph, as he formulates it, excludes every characteristic that is specific and every reference to sexual jouissance. It is true that Freud, because he lacks the category of the signifier, reflects upon this operation, evoking in the following pages the strange oral incorporation, cannibalism, all references to which become useless when we have the notion of identification through the signifier. To speak, as Freud does, of the little boy is to speak of the universal of all the little boys and hence of the universal father, and independently of his link to the mother, therefore independently of his jouissance. I notice as well, Freud himself notes, that it is difficult to give a "concrete metapsychological representation" of this identification. Hence, he does not convoke his myth. For us, that the boy identifies himself with his father cannot be conceived without the signifier of the father. Parenthesis here on the function of this identification: I have for a long time commented on primordial identification with the phallus in Lacan's "On a Question Prior" to stress its crucial function, necessary, of knotting the real to the symbolic, the "ineffable and stupid existence" to the order of the Other, to language and to discourse, from where the little living one can humanise himself. Freud, with this first identification, constitutive of the subject, is on the same terrain.

The two following identifications have this in common, little emphasised but textual, that identifications proper to neurosis, since they are identifications by the symptom – in one case, the cough, in the other, the nervous breakdown – and the symptom implies repression, Freud says it explicitly for both.

As for the second identification, it is sometimes called identification of the unary trait, but this is not it at all. We need to be more precise. Freud says identification by the symptom [*par le symptôme*]. These are cases where it is the symptom that is borrowed, either from the rival or from the Oedipal object. Example: Dora's wrenching cough. He specifies that this is the complete mechanism of the formation of the hysterical symptom and adds that "identification has appeared instead of object-choice" (Freud, [1921] 1955, p. 106). This is an eminently problematic formula, Lacan noted, because it is clear that it is not an identification that masculinises Dora. Also, this is where Freud insists on saying that this identification is only partial, that it borrows only one trait, this trait that Lacan rebaptised as the unary trait. The borrowed unary trait is not that with which she identifies herself; it is that through which she identifies herself, and in this specific case, it is the cough that is the partial trait, the unary trait, and that with which she identifies is her father. But we still need to know how to analyse the symptom, a formation of the unconscious that implies repression. So, the symptom, the cough, once deciphered by Freud, what does it say? Behind the cough, Freud deciphered the sexual thoughts related to her father, the idea of his impotence, and the fantasy of fellatio (or, Lacan adds, of *cuni lingus*), that is to say, oral practises especially useful for the supposedly impotent man. Re-read with Lacan, we understand that underneath the identification of the love object, the father – identification by way of the unary trait of the symptom, which is carried by the signifiers of oral sex, as we call it today – is the identification of desire with desire, of Dora's desire with the desire of the impotent father, just as we have the identification of the beautiful butcher's wife with the supposed desire of her butcher of a husband.

The third identification is another case of identification by the symptom, which, like the first one, does not pass through the object relation. This "identification leaves entirely out of account any object-relation to the person who is being copied" (Ibid., p. 107). Hence a trait in common with the first type of identification. The boarding school girls who witnessed their friend's crisis after receiving a love letter can catch this crisis (the same word that is used for catching the flu [*attraper une grippe*]). The mechanism is the following: one has perceived a significant resemblance, at the level of the relation, she identifies with this point, and the identification is then displaced onto the symptom, the crisis. I quote:

> The identification by means of the symptom has thus become the mark of a point of coincidence between the two egos which has to be kept repressed . . . and . . . it may arise with any new perception of a common quality shared with some person who is not an object of the sexual instinct.
>
> (Ibid., 108)

Lacan has nicely named it "participative identification" proper to hysteria. Freud does not qualify it specifically as hysteric; we will see what authorises us to say this. What is important here is that it is this identification that seems to him to be functioning in the group, "an identification . . . based upon an important emotional common quality" (Ibid.).

This step accomplished, Freud can now go further into the characteristics of the libido of the group. He first comes back to love to once more underline the sexual over-estimation of the object, its idealisation and the self-sacrifice of the ego that accompanies this idealisation. Hence a precise definition of love: an abandonment of the ego in favour of the object that is put in the place of the ego-ideal. What differentiates it from hypnosis is that the hypnotist, certainly equally in the place of the ego-ideal, is not a libidinal object: no sensual tendencies in hypnosis. There lies the point in common with the group: it is a crowd of two [*foule à deux*]; the common trait is not only that an individual is at the place of the ego-ideal, it is that direct sexual tendencies are not there, and Freud dots the i's and crosses the t's, the consideration for the woman is excluded from it, the sexual difference does not intervene here, even when there are women in the group. Let us translate: in the group, the link to the leader, and the reciprocal links between the members, are links of love, not desire of *jouissance*; and even Freud specifies, "love for the woman", which means that for him, love with a sensual aim, "cuts the link to the group" that is proper to the race, nation and class. Lacan does not say anything different when he says that affairs of love are severed "from every social bond" (Lacan, [1974] 1990, p. 38). However, he says more than Freud when he recognises in the third type of identification a hysteric identification. Why hysteric? Because of the exclusion of carnal love since structurally, according to Lacan, lovers, as he calls hysterics, lovers (female or male) are like fish in water when it comes to aim-inhibited tendencies; in other words, they are naturally in the ethics of "outside sex" [*l'éthique* "*hors sexe*"] of desire for desire that love carries. We see that Lacan has a conception of hysteria more elaborate than Freud's.

Note

1 Party fodder [*chair à Parti*], is a pun on both "*chair à canon*" (cannon fodder) and "*chair à pâté*" (patty filling).

References

Freud, S. (1955 [1921]). Group Psychology and the Analysis of the Ego. In: *The Standard Edition of the Complete Psychological Works of Sigmund Freud, Volume XVIII (1920–1922): Beyond the Pleasure Principle, Group Psychology and Other Works* (pp. 65–144). J. Strachey (Trans.). London: Hogarth Press.

Freud, S. (1961 [1923]). The Ego and the Id. In: *The Standard Edition of the Complete Psychological Works of Sigmund Freud, Volume XIX (1923–1925): The Ego and the Id and Other Works* (pp. 1–66). J. Strachey (Trans.). London: Hogarth Press.

Lacan, J. (1990 [1974]). *Television: A Challenge to the Psychoanalytic Establishment.* J. Copjec (Ed.). D. Hollier, R. Krauss, A. Michelson and J. Mehlman (Trans.). New York: Norton.

Lacan, J. (2001 [1970]). Radiophonie. In: *Autres écrits* (pp. 403–447). Paris: Éditions du Seuil.

Lacan, J. (2006 [1945]). Logical Time and the Assertion of Anticipated Certainty. In: *Écrits: The First Complete Edition in English.* B. Fink (Trans.). New York: Norton.

Lacan, J. (2006 [1964]). On Freud's "Trieb". In: *Écrits: The First Complete Edition in English.* B. Fink (Trans.). New York: Norton.

Chapter 10

6th May 2015

I returned to Freud's text in order to tackle the question of group identifications. I had arrived at the third type that he differentiated, the one "based upon an important emotional common quality" (Freud, [1921] 1955, p. 108) and without any particular libidinal link. It is the one that is at work, according to him, between the members of the group.

The principle of cohesion

I won't insist on the definition of the structure of the group. It is already well known. It is "a number of individuals who have put one and the same object in the place of their ego-ideal and have consequently identified themselves with one another in their ego" (Ibid., p. 116). Their affective commonality is thus, in Freud's terms, based on the same love for the same idealised object. This love, as a common factor, is thus the One [*Un*] that homogenises them, and through which each one recognises himself in the others – fraternity – but also to which each one is reduced since the individual differences are at the same time seemingly eclipsed; homogenisation, I could say de-individualisation. If I write a group [*groupe*] of $(a + b + c)$ in which the three letters designate individual differences, once they enter the crowd [*foule*], one can write the transformation produced by the same 'love of/for [*du*] the leader' as a common factor: love $(1 + 1 + 1)$. With the equivocation of the of/for [*de*]: each one loves the leader who is supposed to love each one, and for that leader, each one is ready for all narcissistic renunciation and for every submission. Love is sacrificial; Freud insisted on it. It is the structure of the Freudian group [*foule*], and we can see it is not a set but a class. I will come back to this later.

Freud's text continues beyond this, I will not go into all the details.

I will move on to Freud's amusing developments concerning the differential psychology of the leader, behind whom there is the imagined figure of the hero who takes the place of the primal Father and whom Freud described as one of those self-sufficient beings who loves nobody and whose narcissism is impregnable due to the jouissance that is their lot. One perceives there some fascination on Freud's part. I remind you that he said the same thing about the narcissistic woman who is self-sufficient. Have we ever met one on the couch? The existence of groups where all

DOI: 10.4324/9781032645506-10

individuals are on the same plane and consent to equality, which lowers everyone's claim for the love of the one and only object, the leader, who constitutes the ego-ideal for all, this group shows in any case that – and this is Freud speaking – man is not a herd animal; on this point, he battles against Trotter's thesis. Man is a horde animal. In brief, he wants a leader. If we think of *Totem and Taboo*, he killed one and wants another one. From then on, in the context of the twentieth century, we have retained as essential in this text the critique of the group. This is part of it, but it is not, in my opinion, the most important part of the text.

I underline how Freud insisted on saying that the two identifications, the horizontal one between the members of the group, and the vertical one with the leader, pertain to tendencies inhibited as to their aim. In other words, the object is an object of love but not a sexual object. This is important because further on, in particular in the postscript, Freud underlined what he called "the functional advantage" of the drives inhibited as to their aim, therefore of love as such; only they can create durable links, contrary to "sensual love destined to extinguish itself in satisfaction". And Freud insisted, I quote, "those instincts which are directly sexual incur a loss of energy each time they are satisfied, and must wait to be renewed by a fresh accumulation of sexual libido, so that mean-while the object may have been changed" (Ibid., p. 139). He will add that these tendencies "are unfavourable to the formation of groups" (Ibid., p. 140) which function with the libido inhibited as to its aim". After this, we cannot say that Freud did not perceive, at least at the level of the sexual relation, what, with Lacan, we attribute to jouissance, namely, an anti-social impact, an anti-link, an autistic one, that goes towards the "*Y a de l'Un*". Nor can we say that Freud was not concerned about what makes social links subsist.

His general trajectory is clear. He started looking into the question of links only in 1921. In the beginning, a lot of what he formulated on the pleasure principle and sexual drives had implications for the social link; however, these were not systematically made explicit. Essentially, he thought of libido as linking. The year 1914 is an important date because the forces that go against linking were being highlighted, namely the forces of narcissism. Then in 1920, he reworked his concept of repetition with the discovery of the subject's diabolical attachment to the most painful experience of missed encounters, in other words, jouissance. His thesis about the pleasure principle was refuted as a result, and he had to conclude that there was another force that he named the death drive – improperly named according to Lacan – who used the term jouissance for it, a force that goes against cohesions and attacks the social cement. It is in this analytic context that Freud was interested in groups, rightly because in groups, the social cement is assured. We can grasp how from there on – this is my hypothesis – his aim was not so much to critique groups – this had already been done. Freud, on this point, not only took up the baton, but he said it himself and, in spite of the danger represented by the rise of collectivisms worrying him at the time, his question was about what can cement the collective in spite of its death drive, in other words, what remains of Eros in the group and succeeds in making a cohesion possible thanks to narcissistic renunciation. His response was without ambiguity: only desexualised love can link, whereas jouissance, what he calls the direct sexual drive, separates.

Perhaps there is a balancing effect of history that marks our reading of this text by Freud. When in the twentieth century, we suffered the great tyrannies of totalitarian collectivisms, and when we justly denounce them in the name of the rights of the autonomous, singular individual, of human rights, of democracy and the great ideals of an egalitarian social link, we readily recognise in Freud the precursor who anticipated the disasters of groups [des foules]. However, when we arrive at the start of the twenty-first century, where the individual is reduced to an instrument of the market with all the consequences we experience today, that of corrosion and precariousness of cohesions and links, when we are preoccupied with what conditions what we now call le vivre ensemble [living together], then we see, as I did, that Freud already had a concern about what could constitute a cement between individuals.

The Freudian group is not a discourse

However, there is another question: How far did he (Freud) go into the study of what is a social link? Lacan goes a step further, so it seems to me, probably because of his hypothesis on language as an operator. He situated it at the start as operating upon the individual organism, with the subject-effect and an action upon the body. In writing his four discourses, which are only four because of the four terms programmed by language, S_1, S_2, S, a, he goes beyond Freud with his group.

The difference is that, no matter how numerous the individuals ordered by a discourse-social link, he (Lacan) does not consider them to be a class in which each one is identical to the other; rather, he sees them as a set. Because in a set, there is certainly One of exception that exsists to the set as in the Freudian group. But, the specificity of a set is that it mixes apples and oranges [les torchons et les serviettes] – as we say in French – so it can contain the singularities, and this is what distinguishes it from a class. We recall Lacan's drawings representing the set, taken from Peirce, with different strokes: vertical, oblique and even the absence of strokes in the empty set.

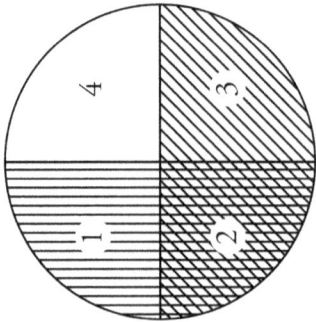

Figure 10.1 Peircian representation of a set

We can say it by playing with words here. In the class constituted by a group, all the strokes lie down, in equivocity with the meaning of "lying down", they lie down even when they believe they are standing. You know the expression "better to die on your feet than live lying down" [*mieux vaut mourir debout que vivre couché*], which – when applied to the Army after we have become enlightened as to its structure – becomes very amusing. One thinks one must die bravely standing up, but only because one has already lain down as a singular subject in front of the idealised master.

I am saying that discourse, according to Lacan, even when it organises a large number, does not constitute them (individuals) into a class because each discourse allows for diverse places. Underneath, there are the places of production (Pro°) and of Truth (T), and in between the two, there is what Lacan calls a barrier of jouissance.

$$\overline{T} \quad || \quad \overline{Pro°}$$

This barrier separates the collectivised forms of jouissance, where all those *apparolés* to this discourse recognise themselves and gather together. On the other side, there is the place of the truth of jouissance that makes each of them singular, not all *apparolés* to discourse. A discourse thus, beyond its effect of homogenisation, accommodates the co-presence of singularities that ultimately arise from the unconscious of each one and from the historical contingencies from which it (the unconscious) is constituted. There is more. Not only does the part below the line write the barrier between production and truth, but the top line distinguishes between the semblance that orders and its other – without capital o – separated by an impossible.

$$\text{Semblance} \rightarrow \text{impossible} \rightarrow \text{other}$$

This other is in the place of that which is at work, respectively the slave, the student, the master signifier and the analysand, but that the same task is shared by individuals who come to occupy the place does not exclude their individual differences.

This top line, therefore, writes a couple marked by an irreducible disparity, master/slave, professor/student, hysteric/master and psychoanalyst/psychoanalysand. Disparity, this term is, by the way, the same one Lacan uses for the transference relationship. We insist on the fact that psychoanalysis is the other side of the master's discourse, yes, because the aim of the latter is to make everyone march at the same pace, whereas the analyst's discourse aims at the opposite, the non-homogenisable singularity of each one. But let us note the master's discourse succeeds in reaching its aim only partially because the objection of singular truths is everywhere. This is the very thing that, according to Freud, clearly appeared in the traumatised soldiers of World War I whom Freud saw as objectors, i.e., subjects who, unbeknownst to themselves, in their unconscious, let's say in their truth, dissented from the imperatives of the master's discourse whereas, for the Army, they were malingerers. Freud said no, "they objected without knowing it".

We see how a discourse distributes clearly diverse phenomena: on the side of the produced jouissance, we may say with Lacan that *our* jouissance, our mode, is on the side of adaptation, of socialisation, and also of collaboration since, without subjects as *apparolés*, a discourse could not exist, and I could say the same of the knowhow [*savoir y faire*] with one's epoch. On the side of truth, we find the individuating difference, the "I" alone, namely, anarchy, the roads that do not lead to Rome as in Georges Brassens' song, thus possible dissidence, if not insurrection in the name of "the truth for which one fights". This is at play in every revolution, says Lacan, but obviously without the real being modified by it, meaning the real of the impossible relationship that all discourses try to make up for via their own real. I quote, "It is that real, when the moment of truth has gone, that will be shaken, until the next crisis", not without "the murkiness of truth being thrown back into darkness" (Lacan, 1970 [2001], p. 443).

All this is to say that for Lacan, a discourse is a link between the dissimilar, between differences; it does not consist simply in being in communication, connected, part of a network, not even as neighbours living in the same space, as we seem to conceive it today. It cannot be defined by regrouping but by the organising, by the articulating of their differences, and this leaves room for a margin of freedom, let's say for a variety of options, more or less subversive, which allows for possible evolutions. Let us note that the page in *Télévision* that Lacan dedicated to the family and the repression attached to it in the anti-master movement of 1968 led up to some remarks about freedom whose shadow does not even subsist in the collectivisms of Eastern countries. As I already said, the implicit part of this development is that the so-called familial repression does not go so far as to leave no possibility for revolt, which happens not only in the act but also starts with a thought.

From this, it clearly appears that the group described by Freud, which one could think corresponds to the master's discourse with its idealised object in place of S_1, is, in reality, different, since it eliminates what constitutes fundamentally the virtue of discourses, namely the coordination of differences. The group is, let's say, a form of degradation (of discourses). Besides, we could think that it is the differences excluded by the fraternal structure of the group that return in the real, in the segregative intolerances for those who do not adjust to it, as Freud well noted. Consequently, fraternity bears all the wars against the "infidels" of all sorts. Obviously, I use the term infidel here as a metaphor.

Links between peers?

Another question is to know how the present forms of universalism promoted by science remain compatible with the social link as defined by Lacan. In today's capitalism, this universalism takes the degraded form of *narcynic* individualism, an expression I used in the past to designate those subjects who, against the backdrop of the roar of the great collective causes of the twentieth century, do not have any other cause but their own jouissance. This type of individualism, under the guise of human rights, aroused the demand for all-out parity at all costs. Parity of rights is surely something deserving of our attention. However, to demand real parity is something different: it is about negating differences in the name of formal equality. Today this goes as far as refusing any distribution of roles in families, at school, and in society. It represents the famous crisis of authority and even claims to impose itself on the difference between the sexes and even on grammar when one chases down the gender of personal pronouns. Regarding these evolutions, Lacan said that the psychoanalyst can only "take stock" [*'dresser constat'*]. A daily clinic of the manifestations of those demands could even be amusing. However, it is not for the psychoanalyst 'to take sides' [*à prendre parti*].

Lacan's position with regard to the question of parity is clear, and one can read to what extent it does not flatter the spirit of the time [*l'air du temps*], if this expression has a meaning. I will try to clarify this. In the first place, Lacan says that every order is regulated by semblances, including the sexual order; there is no discourse that would not be of a semblance. In other words, the social order shapes individuals, and with that, all gender theories could orient themselves, as could some feminists. Everything is organised by semblances, except . . . the other jouissance, which implies [*fait que*] that Sex, the woman, remains the Other – that is, what is not inscribed by the Ones of language – it is therefore always minus one in the order of language, as God himself is the absolute partner. Does the "There is such thing as One" [*Y a de l'Un*] formulated in . . . *Ou pire*, just before Lacan definitively fixed his formulae of sexuation in "L'étourdit", object to what these formulae promote with an implicit, "There is such thing as the Other"? There too, a different kind of feminist could find herself. And Lacan insists on the interest we "should" take in this Other. I leave this question in suspense, to be followed up on some other occasion.

I now go back to parity, or rather to the demand for parity. What could be a social link between peers? In any case, it would not constitute one of the social links constructed by Lacan. Would it be outside discourse? Since it would eliminate the structural impossibility that, in discourse, separates semblance in the position of an agent from its other? Would we have to lower by a notch the definition of social link and say there is a social link as soon as libido goes beyond the limits of the body as such to give value to something that, as an object, is distinct from the subject? Let us remember what Freud said, and I have just evoked: that love between the sexes, self-love, filial love, parental love, friendship, love for humanity, objects, ideas, all of these forms, originally derives from the push toward sexual union. A union that he believed . . . natural. Lacan responds: all established links make up for [*suppléent*] the disunion between the sexes that is there indeed and has nothing natural about it.

I put into tension the Freudian group and Lacan's discourses, but are there any other links that could be outside discourse? This question arose for me a long time ago, based on Lacan's remark about matters of love being split off from established social links, in other words, split off from what he calls discourse. However, what can apparently make more of a link, a link between subjects, a link between bodies, than sexuated love to the point of creating the belief for a moment that there is a sexual relationship, however contingently? This very contingency proves, or at least contributes to demonstrating the impossibility of the relationship, namely that language does not inscribe it; it does not program it. This is the thesis enunciated in *Télévision*. This would not allow us to say that matters of love are outside discourse. This is why I once put forward the notion of an epiphanic discourse to situate them, to use Joyce's famous term.

In any case, certain contemporary groupings [*rassemblements*] demand to be situated according to their structures. Activist associations that rally around a cause, whether it is a humanitarian, a political, or an ecological one, to save the planet or to defend victims in various ways: their structure, whether fleeting or organised, does not pose a question. They have a common cause in the place of a unifying signifier, a common factor for all those who rally around it. Freud would say that they are groups in which the One is not incarnated but can be an abstract idea. However, I think he sufficiently emphasised their difference from groups with a leader: these causes in the position of unifying S_1 – precisely because love of the leader is not required – do not produce the de-individualising submissiveness denounced, for example, in the Army. This is even sometimes their drama; they bump up against the difficulty of finding agreement among individualities. More generally, all cases of solidarity around a task create a link through identification amongst the partners involved in the task and who are not, moreover, libidinally linked. These two types of groupings correspond quite well to what Serge Paugam (2015) describes as two types of links via participation or organisation, either it is elective or organic: elective in the case of a choice for a particular cause and those who serve it, organic when based on the solidarity of work. In both cases, the two pillars of social sentiment, according to Durkheim, namely the need for protection and the need for recognition, are potentially satisfied in it.

All those activist groups prove in any case that capitalism, if it does not make a social link, neither does it impede every social link, and that subjects, as I previously demonstrated, are not all *apparolés* to the values of capitalism. They are all indeed compensatory reactions against the misdemeanours of capitalism, just as the charities of the past were reactions against the misdemeanours of the classical discourse of the master, and their number is increasing in order to support the new victims of our times: the victims of famine, natural disasters, war; the exiled and the asylum seekers; victims of torture and rape; undocumented immigrants, etc.

We can see here that the meaning of what we call "humanitarian" has changed. It used to be in the great epoch of colonisation "humanitarianism on command" ["*humanitairerie de commande*"], i.e., the pseudo humanitarian alibi of "our extortions" (Lacan, [1974] 1990, p. 33), as Lacan says. Today this is all finished, but the effort to repair remains based upon empathy towards the other's suffering and the desire, as they say, to do something useful. It is striking today that politicians regret the decrease in their co-citizens' "political passions" as the latter believe less and less in the causes of political parties. However, it is notable how new causes are invented every day, and even the cause of animals has been added to that of women and children. Without a doubt, they create links based on solidarity between the participants of these activist groups without going through the sacrifice of one's individuality, which is proper to the group with a leader. Whence the question: To what structure of discourse do they correspond?

Before I get there, I want to stop at another type of group that abounds today: the symptom-gatherings. These are all groups that meet in a fleeting or durable fashion, based on a shared taste, or a trait of jouissance, a shared trait of perversion. A common jouissance brings people together, for example, large concerts, or Alcoholics Anonymous, nowadays groups of anorexic, bulimic and even, paradoxically, groups of autistic people among whom the trait that makes them gather is "outside link". At the sexual level, the differentiations increase; we are far from the old binary hetero/homo, sado-maso, queer, trans, and more. All "addicts" (in English in the text) to the same mode of satisfaction. Yet do we not say, "*birds of a feather flock together*" [*qui se ressemble s'assemble*]? This is the formula of the *soft* (in English in the text) voluntary segregation: one separates oneself from what is dissimilar. To which is now added the fact that one may name oneself according to a single characteristic of jouissance. Here, this time, the individuals are really on par. They are identified by a single identity of jouissance, which creates rapprochement, sympathies, and perhaps reciprocal recognition, as unstable as it may be. This link is, all things considered, segregationist by essence: the more one is segregated, the more one segregates oneself as if to keep each other warm. In all these cases, this is not a hidden affective community, thus a repressed one, that makes a link, as Freud said, but obviously a community of symptom-jouissance. So what is the structural difference with the third type of identification in Freud?

This third type is precisely characterised by Freud as being proper to neurosis, implying, therefore, repression, and the trait of identification is the symptom, the crisis among the school girls he spoke about. In *L'insu que sait*, Lacan qualifies it as "participative identification". It is well enunciated, and he says about it: it is hysteric. What justifies saying this? I have already touched on that question, and I will complete it now.

If we take the example of the boarding school, what is going on appears clearly. A boarder enters a crisis after receiving a letter from a man. The others "catch" the crisis. Why? Freud says it is a repressed affective community. Let's say they perceived the desire, an unhappy one here, in relation to the desire of/for a man. Participative identification happens via the mediation of the desire of/for the man [*désir de l'homme*] in its double sense and without knowing anything about the concrete events behind it. Underneath the identification with the crisis of tears, there is an identification with desire: simultaneously with that of the other (the school girl) and with that of the Other (the man of the letter). This is classic if you think of the butcher's wife's identification via the lack of caviar with her friend's lack of salmon, but you know what this identification "wants to say" [*ce que veut dire*] in the unconscious, it says: identification with lack, desire of the Other, the man, the husband in whom everything is satisfied. It is what Freud would call the choice of the drive inhibited as to the aim, and Lacan says: "ethics outside sex" [*éthique hors sexe*].

Can we read something here about the restorative organisations of our times? I evoked empathy, but it can go as far as a participatory identification, as in hysteria, if it passes through the mediation of an implicit relation to the Other. In the classic group, Freud postulates that this mediation is constituted by the need – he even says the illusion – of a Father with a capital F. What would be the mediating term among humanitarian organisations aiming to repair the effects of capitalism? Empathy for the victims is obvious there; however, it does not go without an implicit reference to the impotence of the bio-power of the state, which is now incapable of compensating for the wrongdoings of the capitalist.

Thus three structures. The symptom-group gathers semblables in jouissance (a, a, a . . .). The Freudian group gathers semblables in the relationship with an all-powerful Other A (a, a, a). The hysteric group convokes a barred Other and does not dis-individualise: Ⱥ (a, a', a''). I conclude that it makes a discourse link. By recognising in the third identification described by Freud the participatory identification of hysteric libido, Lacan allows for an accentuation of this perspective. He produces the formula of "participatory identification" in *L'insu que sait,* and a little later, he will say that what he seeks is the "identification to the group". This comment left his followers of the time quite baffled, and this is understandable since Lacan also promoted a psychoanalysis that aimed for, as he said, an "exit from the herd" and produced a lot of criticism about groups. However, the comment indicated that he too, like Freud, had come to be worried about the breakdown of social links.

References

Freud, S. (1955 [1921]). Group Psychology and the Analysis of the Ego. In: *The Standard Edition of the Complete Psychological Works of Sigmund Freud, Volume XVIII (1920–1922): Beyond the Pleasure Principle, Group Psychology and Other Works* (pp. 65–144). J. Strachey (Trans.). London: Hogarth Press.

Lacan, J. (1990 [1974]). *Television: A Challenge to the Psychoanalytic Establishment.* J. Copjec (Ed.). D. Hollier, R. Krauss, A. Michelson and J. Mehlman (Trans.). New York: Norton.

Lacan, J. (2001 [1970]). Radiophonie. In: *Autres écrits* (pp. 449–498). Paris: Éditions du Seuil.

Paugam, S. (2015). *Le lien social*. Paris: Puf.

Chapter 11

20th May 2015

During this second to last session of the year, I think I will linger a little on identifications pertaining to "matters of love" ["*les affaires d'amour*"] before finishing next time by returning to the famous identification with the symptom.

What Lacan designates with this expression – "matters of love" – is not just any love, not the one that possibly unites generations, family members, groups of friends, and all the elective links which, deep down, have in common the exclusion of sex and separate out the feelings of attachment from sexual practice. What is notable is that Lacan includes even the *conjugo* among these. The term is interesting in that it suspends the instituted forms, be it marriage, civil union, or other, and retains only the idea of the couple's constancy. According to Lacan, it is the same for the Greek *philia,* which seems to eliminate the *sexuated* dimension to the benefit, fundamentally, of companionship. These are forms in which what is at stake is instead "the law of the dwelling" (Lacan, [1974] 1990, p. 39), that is, domestic economy. Obviously, the actual forms of marriage in which matters of love and household overlap can hardly be included in this Lacanian distribution.

Dialectic of phallic identifications

In any case, right from the start and following Freud, Lacan posed the question of the function of identifications in sexuated identity, in being a man or being a woman. Freud's Oedipean little story [*historiole*] – so I name it in order to distinguish it from his myth of Totem and Taboo – that unfolds between the four walls of a house he uses in order to give an account of the fact that a subject identifies itself to its anatomical sex, real, the little girl to the woman, the little boy to the man, at least when he or she identifies with it, and he situates as symptomatic all that constitutes an obstacle to this conforming identification. In this sense, for Freud, the reality of anatomy makes destiny; it commands. But, at the same time, the necessary character of those identifications with the symbols and images of the Oedipean man and woman clearly indicates that Freud knew that anatomy was not sufficient to orient erotic tastes, that is, libido. His notion of bisexuality attests to it, and one can say that today's mores bring a striking confirmation of it.

DOI: 10.4324/9781032645506-11

Lacan took it from there, remaining within the Freudian axis. However, in the years of his return to Freud, he both unfolded and displaced this conceptualisation by relating the whole problematic of sexuated identity, with what it includes of the drives, to the phallic signifier, and by reformulating the difference between the sexes and their relations based only on the phallic dialectic. However, the phallus is not simply the signifier of the lack of desire – I insisted on it – but also the signifier of jouissance. There is a reservation already from that time. He says, I quote:

> It is appropriate to investigate whether phallic mediation exhaustively accounts for everything drive-related that can manifest itself in women, especially the whole current of maternal instinct. Why not posit here that the fact that everything that is analyzable is sexual does not mean that everything that is sexual is accessible to analysis?
>
> (Lacan, [1962] 2006, p. 614)

What we have here could be called a stepping stone [*pierre d'attente*] toward future developments on the woman, but perhaps more broadly on sexuality.

In the meantime, as we know, he distributes the sexes between having or being the phallus, which regulates the bond in a couple at the level of love as well as at the level of desire. All developments in "The Direction of the Treatment", "The Signification of the Phallus" and "Guiding Remarks for a Convention on Female Sexuality" unfold this construction by showing how this "peerless" ["*sans pair*"] signifier sustains the couple of love and of desire and does so differently on the side of man and on the side of woman.

I summarise the thesis concerning phallic mediation that Lacan evokes again in "L'étourdit". In his relationship with woman, man satisfies his demand for love, whose call is "to be the phallus". He satisfies it as far as the woman's phallic lack constitutes her as giving in love what she does not have. But his own desire of the phallus is not exhausted in this relation, and it diverges towards an "other woman", "who may signify this phallus in various ways, either as a virgin or as a prostitute" (Lacan, [1966] 2006, p. 583) and he will also add the phallus-girl. On the side of a woman in her relationship with a man, an experience of love converges on the same object, which as such, deprives her of what she is giving. However, when it comes to her desire, "she finds the signifier of her own desire in the body of the person to whom her demand for love is addressed" (Ibid.). However, this does not make her devoted to an attachment "without duplicity"; he underlines and accentuates it in "Guiding Remarks . . .". Beyond her love for the man who is provided with an organ, "it is a castrated lover or a dead man (or the two in one)" (Lacan, [1962] 2006, p. 617) who calls for her adoration.

One must add that, according to the Lacan of that time, the desire to be the phallus characterises the neurotic in general. The formula accentuates the dimension of the demand for love to the detriment of carnal desire. It is a wish, not an identification, and whether male or female, says Lacan, the neurotic must discover that he or she is not it. I evoke here the last chapter of "The Direction of the Treatment"

(Lacan, [1961] 2006, p. 536). It is impossible to really be the lack of the Other, and this is true for all speaking beings independently of their sex, but in the sexual game, the feminine partner insofar as she is constituted by the man's desire, which is desire of/for [*du*] the phallus (which implies what the mother lacked) is, in fact, phallicised. It is for him that she is the phallus. Being desired phallicises a woman via the mediation of the Other, the man. It is "for what she is not" (that is the phallus) that a woman "expects to be desired as well as loved" (Lacan, [1966] 2006, p. 583). From then on, we understand that the neurotic wish "to be the phallus" more easily comes to redouble in a woman the place that she occupies in the couple.

One can see this distribution is not an essentialist one; it is via the mediation of the Other that each one is distinguished in terms of having or being, hence the term dialectic. On the side of women, what would it mean, for example, "to be the phallus" in the couple, without the masculine Other? As I already underlined, one is the phallus for the other, not per se [*en soi*]. However, one could not say the same about the man having the phallus, except that he has it only by way of an effect of castration which, I quote, "presupposes the subjectivity of the Other as the locus of its law" (Lacan, [1962] 2006, p. 616). It is in that sense that he is an effect of discourse.

Unconscious desire and genitality

In any case, this whole dialectic concerns love and desire. In these paragraphs that I have reiterated, what is missing is the register of corporeal jouissance of the sexual orgasm. How was this approached at that time? The response given is very precise: "that the genital act must find its place in desire's unconscious articulation is the discovery of analysis" (Lacan [1961] 2006, p. 529). Hence the genital act is supposed to be subordinated to the dialectic of the subject and the Other, and two very precise examples are constructed from that idea. The first one concerns his theory of feminine frigidity in 1958.

In "The Signification of the Phallus" and "Guiding Remarks . . .", Lacan indicates that frigidity supposes the whole neurotic structure, even if it appears outside the fabric of the symptoms: "that it is refractory to all somatic treatments and, on the other hand, for the usual failure of the dedicated efforts [*bons offices*] of the most desired partner. Analysis alone mobilises it" (Lacan, [1962] 2006, p. 616). A big promise, isn't it? How does it mobilise it? "It is in this respect that an un-veiling of the Other involved in the transference can modify a symbolically com-manded defense" (Ibid.). Thus the idea that frigidity is located in the dimension of a defense and even of "masquerade" which operates in relation to the Other, a masquerade as nothing more than an adjustment to the Other's requirements.

"Guiding Remarks" further specifies this. Desire is desire of the Other. Hence, in the subject's unconscious, what is present is the desire of the Other, that is, the phallus desired by the mother. I have said it already, for man, beyond the "You are my wife" ["*Tu es ma femme*"] that elects one as his, his desire for the phallus manifests itself via the girl-phallus, or "the other woman". And here, besides, is the secret of the function of the other woman for the woman hysteric, as we see it in the case of the butcher's wife! For a woman – beyond the man whose "attributes she cherishes", that is to say, the man with a penis – hence behind the veil, her desire for the phallus erects what Lacan calls the "ideal incubus", that is, the castrated lover or the dead man. And he adds: "it is because of this ideal incubus that an embrace-like receptivity must be displaced in a sheath-like sensitivity onto the penis" (Ibid., p. 617). "Sensibility of a sheath": here is an implicit hypothesis on feminine orgasm! With this sheath, one is not far from the geometry of the glove of which Lacan says in *Le sinthome* that it is all we have to represent the sexual relation which is lacking. But here, he supposed more than the imaginary representation: that everything happens as if the glove loves the finger. He adds, in effect: it is to this sheath-like sensibility that, I quote: "is thwarted by any imaginary identification a woman may have (as her stature as an object offered up to desire) with the phallic standard [*étalon*] that props up fantasy" (Ibid.). Here is, in any case, the causality of frigidity: "An identification with the phallic standard", that is, the erected phallus. One cannot state more clearly the hypothesis of the subordination of the jouissance of the sexual act to the subjective problematic. Suffice it to say that, in trying to be the phallus, it would be better if she were only the semblance [*semblant*] of it.

Another example is the case of the three-card Monte man in "Direction of the Treatment". He puts this case in parallel with that of the butcher's wife, which illustrates not feminine orgasm but the desire of the hysteric. Regarding this man thus affected by temporary impotence, one can see Lacan's reading: the sexual act, the exercise of virile potency which was impeded, is given back to him by his mistress' manoeuver, when she tells him about her dream in which her own phallic lack was sufficiently evident to restore his powers. Here again, the example serves to demonstrate that the act is subordinated to the dialectic of the relation to the Other. In this case, Lacan makes explicit that, as a neurotic, he wants to be the phallus and, in showing him she does not have it, she restores for him the conditions for exercising his fantasy.

The postulate of these constructions, which we have great difficulty getting rid of, is that the so-called genital jouissance is thought to be subordinated to what operates in the symbolic. Similarly, for a long time, Lacan postulated that the symbolic ordered the imaginary, S/I, that is what he inscribed in his R schema, and likewise, the symbolic at stake in the relation of the subject to the Other is supposed to determine the vicissitudes of the real sexual jouissance, S/R. The analytic promise was therefore strongly reinforced in the hope that analysis could cure the sexual symptoms: masculine impotence in its various forms and feminine frigidity. Up until *Encore,* one finds enunciated the promise, even the promise that goes beyond that of orgasm. Analysis, Lacan says, can (I say can and not must) "sometimes" lead to the possibility that "each one properly fucks his own [*sa chacune*], in other words, analysis can lead to the fact that the same object, the one [*la une*] in question, be at the same time cause of desire and condition of jouissance in 'the successful sexual act'" (Lacan, [1974] 1990, p. 38) as he says in *Télévision*. Thus a promise to cure what Freud named "the debasement" [*ravalement*] of sexual life. The expressions "it can" and "sometimes" indicate the possibility of it, nothing is for sure then, and one can understand why. It is that the so-called "each one" [*une chacune*] depends on the encounter, *Tuché*. This cannot be programmed, however it happens, sometimes, via a modified relation to the Other.

Jouissance of the body . . .

The question that Lacan poses at the beginning of *Encore*, namely, where does the jouissance of the body of the Other come from, clearly shows what these constructions leave out, if I may say so. Accounting for the possibility of the couple by way of desire does not account for the jouissance of bodies. That the question is posed regarding the jouissance of the Other as body sufficiently indicates that the phallic dialectic of desire and love did not account for it. Here we could not say any more than what he said in the 60s, that it is an effect of the relation to the barred Other, A, upon which, indeed, analysis can operate. A change of postulate is implied: the jouissance of the Other as body does not stem from the subjective dialectic. In other words, to use the terms I already quoted: the unconscious articulation of desire is not sufficient to account for the so-called genital jouissance, which therefore is not commanded by the various identifications already evoked.

The table that Lacan presents on page 73 of *Encore* in applying the formulae of sexuation does not constitute an objection to what I am underlining.

This table simply indicates how the heterosexual couple is structured when it occurs. The man, what we can call man, is identified by the phallus with a capital P, correlated to the phallic jouissance, which implies castration. It is such only via discourse because "only discourses exist". It is, therefore, not about man in a

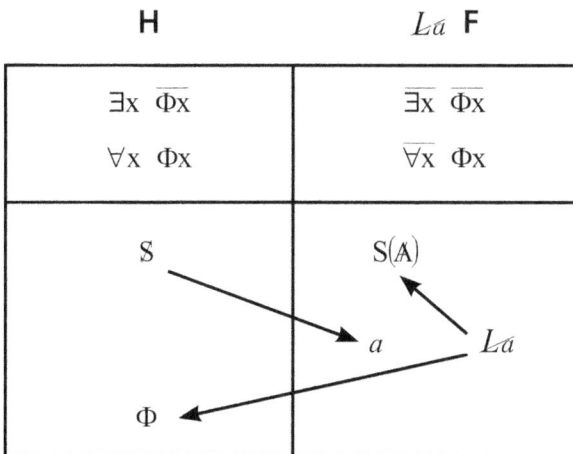

Figure 11.1 Table of sexuation

generic sense; it is not all males; it is man as an effect of discourse, supported by the phallic semblance, who is in relation to desire only via his object *a*. It is the writing of the "a-sexuated" [*a-sexué*]. On the other side, the writing of the barred woman shows that there is no instituting identification of the woman in discourse. She is the absolute Other. Two ways are open to her desire as a subject, one towards the phallus, which presides over the hetero couple through everything I have evoked about the phallic dialectic and masquerade, the other one towards S(A̶), the hole in the Other of language. This is to say that a woman, even if she is heterosexual, is not all heterosexual. I underline two points: first of all, these formulae do not write a heterosexual norm, but only a possibility. They indicate what could cement a couple and, on the other hand, they say nothing about the question initially posed: where does the jouissance of the body of the Other come from, the body that symbolises it? They only tell us what presides over the rapprochement of bodies.

What body?

What body does he speak about here? The speaking body theorised by Lacan up until then was contained in one formula: it is the "locus of the Other" (Lacan, [1973b] 2001, p. 418). And what is the result of that taking hold of the Other, of that incorporation? It is twofold: the body is a "desert of jouissance" through the effect of the signifying negativisation. However, for it (the body), metonymy is the rule, which ensures the drifting of the jouissance of the drives, which are an effect of the saying [*dire*] of demand. Lacan said it again differently. The unconscious affects not the subject but the body (Lacan, [2011] 2018, p. 218) and the subject of the unconscious, the latter being supposed to the unconscious that ciphers jouissance, "gears into [*embraye sur*] the body" (Lacan, [1974] 1990, p. 37). This is the definitive thesis in Lacan, and the Borromean knot keeps to this same line. It thus posits a hiatus between desire and jouissance, which is proper to the one who speaks (*le parlant*) and is not about debasement [*ravalement*] as a particular symptom.

The Ratman makes this perceptible. His obsession fixates some jouissance of the anal drive in the fantasy of his relation to the lady and to the father. With the end of his obsession, he is not cured. He is not cured of his anxiety about the desire of the Other, but there is more to it; we do not know anything about his genital jouissance, about his relation to the absolute Other of sex, let us say how the jouissance of the Other as body is determined. Freud does not even open this chapter.

I summarise: the body as the locus of the Other is the locus of a jouissance fitted out [*appareillée*] by language, phallic and drive jouissance, which does not make a relation of jouissance with the other sex; it is the body of the a-sexuated. How does it have access to the body of the partner-Other? First response: via its perverse traits, its unary traits of jouissance. See in *Radiophonie* the example of *Bel-Ami* and the metonymy, which makes the jouissance of the oyster drift to the ear of the woman.

Encore evokes the body that "symbolises the Other". This is a new formula, and in it, the Other in question is not the same. It is not that of language. The Other that the body symbolises, let us say, represents, is, I quote *Télévision*, "the radical

Other, evoked by the nonrelation embodied by sex" (Lacan, [1974] 1990, p. 40) and which is written S(A̶), the hole in the Other of language. This body is not *the* feminine body; it is *a* feminine body because it is not the body without a penis of all women since it is not every woman who, with her body, symbolises the Other for a man. Lacan has always been categorical on that point: the woman is the absolute Other of the phallic One. Well before the 70s and his formulae of sexuation he said that there is the woman only as excluded from the nature of things, which is the nature of discourse; excluded from discourse, she represents the absolute Other for the man. This thesis already figures in "Guiding Remarks . . ." where it is said that "she represents the absolute Other in the phallocentric dialectic" (Lacan, [1962] 2006, p. 616). From that, we understand that the difference between the sexes is conceived as a point of resistance not reducible to the demand for parity. By definition, parity excludes the Other even more radically than the discourses. This is why it is very interesting to study how the Other has been treated in history. It is part of a long series of what appears nowadays as domination, devaluing discrimination, racism. In that regard, segregation could almost be a lesser evil.

The unlikely body

So, finally, what is the reply to the question posed at the beginning of *Encore,* which does not pertain to just any jouissance but precisely to the jouissance of the sexual relation? The response is not made explicit in this seminar. At the end of that year, Lacan simply reformulates the impasse of the sexual non-relation and its correlate, which is generalised perversion, saying that the "jouissance of the Other taken as a body is always inadequate – perverse, on the one hand, insofar as the Other is reduced to object a, and crazy and enigmatic, on the other, I would say" (Lacan, [1975] 1999, p. 144).

A more precise response is nevertheless developed in this seminar in the form of various innovative contributions. I have already said the most innovative one is not what he advances about women with the formulae of sexuation, which simply completes what was already there in "L'étourdit". The most innovative is the relation between language and jouissance. On the relation between language and jouissance, the seminar takes up again and, first of all, clarifies a thesis that was already present previously, saying, "reality is approached with apparatuses of jouissance" (Ibid., p. 55), that is, the linguistic apparatus. In other words, the apparatus of jouissance is the same as the apparatus of knowledge [*connaissance*]. It is what I called Lacan's anti-cognitivist hypothesis, cognitivism having made its entry into psychoanalysis with Anna Freud, when she supposes in the child three independent lines of development: that of the object relation, of the drives and of knowledge [*connaissance*] as if thinking were autonomous from libido. Lacan's sentence that I just quoted simply reformulates his hypothesis: language attains something other than itself, namely the living individual, which is the same as the one we call the subject of the unconscious. The subject of the unconscious is the body fitted [*appareillé*] by language. This is thus a reprise of a prior thesis.

What is new, however, is to posit that the signifier enjoys itself [*se jouit*]. This is a subversion of the notion of knowledge [*savoir*], hence: "the unconscious is the fact that being, by speaking, enjoys" (Ibid., p. 104–105), and "jouissance is in the ciphering" (Lacan, 2001, p. 556) and the "I think enjoys itself" ["*le je pense se jouit*"]. Therefore, this is the end of the heteronomy of the two dimensions of language and jouissance. And the real formula of the response to the question at the beginning of *Encore* comes soon after, with the thesis of the symptom-partner. This extends to the sexual partner the thesis on the symptom in general, enunciated at the beginning of "R.S.I", that of the partner-symptom. It says that the "*fixion*" with an "x", let us say the fixation of jouissance that is the symptom is made by way of an element of the unconscious or on an element of the unconscious that Lacan names letter, which is identical to itself because it is disjointed from any semantics but nonetheless enjoyed. Hence the formula "you enjoy (from) your unconscious" [*vous jouissez de votre inconscient*], in other words, the symptom in its general-ised definition is some knowledge [*c'est du savoir*], some enjoyed *lalangue* [*de lalangue jouie*]. This places the symptom outside the signifying chain, thus, it is an exception outside sense, and it makes of the real unconscious the true partner. This thesis can even be applied to the jouissance of the sexual act itself. And Lacan asks: What is a woman for a man? She is a symptom (Lacan, 1975). Here I remind you of the precisions I had to bring to the notion of the real unconscious. The real unconscious is the language-unconscious; there is no such thing as the language-unconscious on the one side and the real unconscious on the other side. The thesis of the language-unconscious is constant in Lacan, except that he first thought of this language-unconscious as a chain of discourse that represents the subject; it is the graph of desire. Later, he will approach it – in the developments I am evoking – at the level of the elements coming from *lalangue,* which do not make a chain but mark the body. Hence for example, his question: How does an element of *lalangue* precipitate into language? Answer: via jouissance. The proof is found in the deci-phering of the unconscious, which is certainly only "a lucubration of knowledge [*savoir*] upon *lalangue*" but which attests to the incidence of the latter upon the enjoying body. Hence, the symptom as the enjoyed letter makes the unconscious exist in the real, and this symptom is a partner to the a-substantial subject of the chain. If one tried to situate it in the writing of the analytic discourse, it would be S_2, some enjoyed knowledge [*savoir*] in the place of truth. "La Troisième" affirms that the symptom comes from the real. In effect, and in a double way, from the real of the impossible relation which it makes up for and from the real of life without which there would not be any jouissance. There where Lacan wrote $S◊a$, where *a* is the object cause of desire, one could write a variation of it which completes it: $S◊Σ$ where the symptom as "event of the body" is jouissance. Here we have an answer to the question at the beginning of *Encore*: Where does the jouissance of the Other as a body come from? It does not come from the Other itself; it comes from the unconscious, from the One, as a sort of partner interposed between the One and the Other. Hence the affirmation in "La Troisième" that says that what he writes in the knot as jouissance of the barred Other J(A̶) does not exist, or in any case, it does not exist in the objective sense of the *of* [*de*].

This formula of the partner-symptom is thus equivalent to the sexual partner of the One, the man, when it is a woman. And Lacan dots the i's in his second conference on Joyce: "Individuals . . . can be symptoms themselves only in relation to other bodies. For example, a woman is symptom of another body" (Lacan, [1987] 2001, p. 569). Therefore, a body as a symptom of another body. This goes not only for neurosis but for all cases of heterosexuality, where the body symbolises the Other. The question is to know if we should perhaps add that this is proper, not only to heterosexuality but to any sexual partner, since there is no other partner than the symptom; and that, for example, the gadgets of civilisation are themselves suppletive symptoms of the (non) relation.

I have often insisted on the question of how to use these theses in analytic practice itself. The fact the symptom comes from the real and not from truth necessarily poses a question for psychoanalysis. In effect, as I already said, it started from the opposite postulate with Freud, in what we called his psychology of love life – except that Freud, contrary to Lacan, did not problematise the jouissance proper to the sexual relation but only that of neurotic symptoms. The symptom coming from the real means that there is no psychology, not so much the psychology of love life – the expression is too vague – but of the symptom jouissance, the latter resulting from the way *lalangue* precipitated into a letter, "fixion" of jouissance. Hence Lacan's formula in his "Preface to the English Edition of Seminar XI": "the little we know about the real shows its antinomy to all verisimilitude". This is true of the real of life in general, but it also applies to the symptom as real and coming from the real of those who speak. Sense, insofar as it comes from "the instance of the letter" as Lacan specifies in *The Sinthome*, sense can nourish it and even make it prosper or extinguish it (he says), at least in part. However, if the true sense of a symptom is the real, it is the real that accounts for it. This is to say, as I formulated a long time ago: there is no subject without a symptom as a solution to the non-relation, and therefore, the so-called therapeutic effect on the symptom, for example, the undeniable disappearance of the Ratman's obsession, is simply a change in symptom. It is here that the notion of identification with the symptom, upon which I will finish this year's teaching, becomes necessary.

References

Lacan, J. (1975). *R.S.I. Seminaire XXII (1974–1975) leçon du 21 Janvier 1975* [Unpublished manuscript].

Lacan, J. (1990 [1974]). *Television: A Challenge to the Psychoanalytic Establishment.* J. Copjec (Ed.). D. Hollier, R. Krauss, A. Michelson and J. Mehlman (Trans.). New York: Norton.

Lacan, J. (1999 [1975]). *The Seminar of Jacques Lacan, Book XX: Encore, On Feminine Sexuality, The Limits of Love and Knowledge 1972–1973.* B. Fink (Trans.). New York: Norton.

Lacan, J. (2001 [1973a]). Introduction à l'édition allemande d'un premier volume des Écrits. In: *Autres écrits* (pp. 553–559). Paris: Éditions du Seuil.

Lacan, J. (2001 [1973b]). L'étourdit. In: *Autres écrits* (pp. 449–498). Paris: Éditions du Seuil.

Lacan, J. (2001 [1987]). Joyce le symptòme. In: *Autres écrits* (pp. 565–570). Paris: Éditions du Seuil.

Lacan, J. (2006 [1961]). The Direction of the Treatment and the Principles of Its Power. In: *Écrits: The First Complete Edition in English*. B. Fink (Trans.). New York: Norton.

Lacan, J. (2006 [1962]). Guiding Remarks for a Convention on Female Sexuality. In: *Écrits: The First Complete Edition in English*. B. Fink (Trans.). New York: Norton.

Lacan, J. (2006 [1966]). The Signification of the Phallus. In: *Écrits: The First Complete Edition in English*. B. Fink (Trans.). New York: Norton.

Lacan, J. (2018 [2011]). *The Seminar of Jacques Lacan, Book XIX: . . . Or Worse 1971–1972*. A. R. Price (Trans.). Cambridge: Polity Press.

Chapter 12

3rd June 2015

Identification with the symptom

I have thus shown last time that to the partner, as he first conceived it, beginning from the signifier phallus, then the object a, both of which accounted for desire, Lacan added the partner-symptom, which includes the register of real jouissance.

By real jouissance, I mean the one that is not *jouis-sens*. From this, we understand that, even when he said later, "they authorize from themselves, the sexuated beings" (Lacan, 1974), this "themselves" is not the subject represented by its speech [*parole*] but by its jouissance-symptom, "*extimate*", that comes to him via the knowledge of *lalangue*, that hits the target on his body, thus making language pass to the real. This "*extimate*" is in him, but it is not him; it does more than divide him by redoubling his signifying split [*refente*]; it parasitises him. I could say just like a tapeworm, because you will have noticed that in saying a woman is a symptom for a man, right after having redefined the symptom as a function of the letter, Lacan does not develop the consequences, but there is far more to it. Indeed, what this points to is that, in spite of the non-relation, we nonetheless happily imagine that we are in a link between two, an imagining that must be so dear to us that even Freud himself ascribed to Eros the One of fusion. And thus, when Lacan says woman-symptom – there where we imagine at least a conjunction of jouissances – he says there is only one, the autistic jouissance of the One coupled with its unconscious. Hence, the formulae: you enjoy of/from [*de*] your unconscious, the symptom is the way we enjoy of/from [*de*] the unconscious, the word has become an object, even in bed, as I indicated last time. Hence, we understand that the jouissance of the Other – objective genitive – does not exist.

There where we believed there was One and the Other, the One misses the Other and remains with the One of its unconscious. The "There is such a thing as One" ["*Y a de l'Un*"] insisted on in . . . *Ou pire* is therefore redoubled: there is the One-saying of the One that knows itself all alone (Lacan, [2011] 2018, p. 218) and the One of symptom-jouissance, opaque jouissance, Lacan insists, *extimate* its only partner.

DOI: 10.4324/9781032645506-12

Non extimate jouissance

However, not all jouissance is opaque. That of fantasy – to be written *jouis-sens* in two words – is not opaque. On the contrary, it constitutes a quilting point for the half-said of its truth. Admittedly, it remains unnoticed by the subject, and all the work of an analysis is required so he can see the function of its "absolute signification", which occludes the bar on the Other and measures the extent of his confidence in it, about which he himself had no idea. Signification belongs to the imaginary, but the term '"absolute", which refers to its constancy, is what makes it swerve towards the real. *The Logic of Fantasy*, as its title indicates, is aimed at specifying its place in the structure of language, homologous to a postulate in logic, the latter being a proposition outside the system that conditions all the demonstrable propositions of the system. Equally, fantasy conditions all the sayings of truth [*dits de vérité*] of the subject and, as varied as these are, fantasy itself does not fluctuate. It is, therefore, in the place of the real insofar as it is always in the same place. The reference to the torus aimed at giving the topology of this place, but it did not imply that fantasy was real, in a strong sense, that is outside the symbolic and the imaginary. Fantasy is the most real of sense; it is one-way [*sens unique*], as I said it is, in a way, congealed sense. When Lacan later evoked the One of sense, this refers, I believe, to the fantasy that remains homogenous to the subject with the jouissance of the drive lodged within. The jouissance of the drive is imperative, if not irrepressible but it is not opaque; not only does it come from demand, but it also has its signifiers, it drifts into metonymy, one hears it and recognises it, it even has its clubs, and in neurosis, it is the vehicle of demand addressed to the Other. It also has a subjective function; it is through it, through the activity of the drives that the subject operates with his loss, says Lacan. The fantasy is the jouissance that sticks to the subject, holds it and likes it [*tient à lui*]; and why is this? Because fantasy is not jouissance of the body, it is always jouissance of a representation of jouissance of the body. Besides, look at Freud's trajectory. He started from the symptoms in the plural, which, based on deciphering, are interpreted as the return of the repressed drives. He became aware of the presence of the fantasy only later, and he spoke about it outside the symptomatic frame [*trame*], calling more for a construction than an admission, as if it were impossible to say. What is the impossible to say of a fantasy? "A child is being beaten", which is the Freudian model, is *said*, a phrase, but what is not said in this *said* is its erogenous function. Equally, the Ratman's scenario of the anal effraction of the body by the rat of the Other, what he misrecognises [*méconnait*] is the erogenous function of this representation; "pleasure of his own of which he himself was unaware", says Freud (Freud [1909] 1955, p. 167).

In fantasy, one enjoys the representation of jouissance, and representation is the opposite of opacity; it [*ça*] even claims to make the real pass to the visible, to the scopic, to representation. With fantasy, one remains in the field of "mentality" in accordance with the fact that the body – in compliance with the mirror stage [*stade du miroir oblige*] – is introduced into the economy of jouissance via the imaginary.

The fantasy, therefore, adds to the subject represented by the signifier, to the One that knows itself all alone, a representation of jouissance. The "Direction of the Treatment" spoke of an image in which a subject can hold itself accountable, and we would not say identification with the fantasy because the subject is identified via its fantasy or rather via the object lodged at the heart of its fantasy. The "Proposition of 67" on the pass is constructed upon this presupposition.

Nevertheless, with the opaque jouissance of the symptom, Lacan introduced something else, the notion of a jouissance without representation, outside mentality. About it, we can say that its real "shows its antinomy to all verisimilitude" that it is outside the symbolic and outside the imaginary. It does not come from the truth of the subject, but from the real. A threshold is crossed here: without representation but eventually not without words, not without an element of language passed to the real. In the jouissance of the text *Finnegans Wake*, this *lalenglish* [*lalanglaise*] has become a partner, and this is true of any symptom of the unconscious. It is jouissance of the letter, by definition identical to itself (which does not say what its One is, I will get back to this). And insofar as it is identical to itself, it is an exception in relation to the signifier never identical to itself (Lacan, 1975), but beyond that, it is outside representation. In other words, it consists of the enjoyment of the linguistic matter without discourse, without the representations and the narratives of discourse. This symptom is a "*fixion*" (with an *x* of unconscious knowledge [*savoir*]), that is some *lalangue* passed to the real of jouissance, according to its definition in *Encore*. This jouissance is, however, not jouissance of life, and it is for that very reason that Lacan wonders in "La Troisième" about a possible jouissance of life. We do not know anything about the latter; we can only imagine it, we think we recognise it in the cat's purr, and we can ask, with Lacan, whether the lily of the field enjoys it. It is an unfathomable question because nothing of what has been named belongs to life anymore, life with a capital L. Language fixes jouissance and at the same time mortifies it. It makes "dead wood"of it, says Lacan. In this sense, neither in its usage of living language nor in the *lalangue* symptom is there ever any jouissance of life, although one needs the living body in order to enjoy.

I go back to the symptom to mark the path travelled from Freud to Lacan. Freud first perceived without naming the effects of the unconscious on the body; he detected them with the discovery of the drives and also of phallic jouissance. As for the Other jouissance, it was, for him, a point of interrogation until the end. He posed the symptom simply as a return of the drives. Lacan kept the definition of the symptom: it is a fixation of jouissance. But having grasped the linguistic nature of the unconscious, he drew from it this consequence: no sexual relation. This allowed him to make the function of the symptom that Freud did not see appear: it makes up [*supplée*] for the relationship that is lacking. It is, therefore, not proper to neurosis but a fact of structure, no subject without symptom. From the start, he formulated it as a formation of the language-unconscious, precisely a metaphor for the signifier of the trauma, as he said in "The Instance of the Letter in the Unconscious". Thus the operation of deciphering that metaphor in accordance with the Freudian practice should, in the end, allow the signifier of the original traumatic jouissance to be revealed. We rather often repeat that Lacan passed from the symptom meta-phor to the symptom letter, but well before this last formulation, there is a rupture in this problem, and it is clearly legible when he says: the unconscious ciphers jouissance, and "in the ciphering is the jouissance" (Lacan, [1973] 2001, p. 556), the one we call phallic, effect of "the encounter between speech and the body", the one we decipher in analysis. On page 19 of *Télévision*, Lacan makes this differ-ence very explicit: the deciphering is not a purely linguistic way of accessing the revelation of an experience of jouissance; the ciphering/deciphering *is* jouissance. The exact formulation in *Télévision* is: "the jouissance that Freud implies through the term primary process properly consists in the logical straits through which he so artfully leads us" (Lacan, [1990] 1974, p. 9). Later, in *Les non dupes errent*, he evokes the elements of *lalangue* that remain undeciphered as so many bits of jouis-sance, thus, he supposes a coalescence between the symbolic of *lalangue* and the real jouissance. Real, but nevertheless not the simple jouissance of life, as I said. With this coalescence, with the enjoyed knowledge [*savoir joui*], it is the end of the two heteronomous fields that he still had to differentiate in "Lituraterre", that of language and that of the living, as I said, the letter supposed to participate in both, making a borderland [*bord*] between them. As a result, the question is again posed of situating the symptom in relation to deciphering, from which it is distinguished by its fixity; and the question is posed of the One of the symptom.

Of the real ones

The difference between the Borromean knot of "La Troisième" and that of *RSI* is, in that regard, very instructive. In both cases, the symptom is a mix of real and symbolic, outside the imaginary. But Lacan first placed it in the symbolic as an overflow of the ring of the real into the symbolic. In this, we were left with the hope that through the symbolic, through interpretation itself playing with *lalangue*, we could reduce it. Then he corrects himself, which indicates, by the way, that Lacan is not constructing a dogma but fumbles in simply trying to think psychoanalysis. So, he places it there where it must be, as an overflow of the symbolic into the real outside sense. It alone is opaque and, more than that, a parasite. Indeed, it is in this way that the subject perceives what we call his symptoms as something that is in him, that inconveniences him, but is not him. The notion of identification with the symptom comes from there. Lacan does not make of it a prescription for the end of analysis. He says it is the best we can do, and it comes perhaps with a "know-how" [*savoir y faire*], in other words, to manage it [*s'en débrouiller*] at the least cost. This is a bit abridged, he adds, nothing more than a therapeutic effect coming from a change, not in the symptom, but in the subject. The identification with the symptom is not an operation that concerns the subject of the unconscious if the subject of the unconscious is the one who "gears into the body" (Ibid., p. 37), as he says in *Télévi-sion*, that is the subject supposed to the unconscious insofar as it is an apparatus of jouissance. It is an operation that concerns rather the subject of truth, the one we listen to and which is also a consciousness of self [*conscience de soi*], and which is rightly affected by its unconscious knowledge, I could say by the symptoms of its unconscious knowledge. This subject, at the entry to analysis, is conscious of suffering from this or that symptom, conscious during the analysis of stumbling up against the impotence of truth as half-said, conscious of not being able to arrive at rectifying the insufficient jouissance, the one that is not it, the phallic one, and also of not being able to eliminate the parasite.

The expression "identification with the symptom" poses a prior question, a major question for psychoanalysis, I believe: Can we identify our symptom, I mean the letter of our symptom, even its knotting with *jouis-sens*? We can identify fantasy, yes, let's say rather circumscribe it since it causes the going round and round of the analysand's speech [*la parole analysante*]. No doubt about it, the individual experiences of analysands converge in attesting to this. What is at stake in the question I pose is very practical: What can put an end to the analytic deciphering? The question is posed because the unconscious that ciphers phallic jouissance, the one that has the function of a subject says Lacan, this unconscious is a worker that never goes on strike, but this does not prevent this other worker, the analysand, from wanting to hand in his notice. On this point, Lacan formulated a first response in "L'introduction à l'édition allemande des Ecrits" in 1973: sense, and here sense is the fantasy, puts an end to the deciphering but the two dimensions, deciphering and sense, are heterogenous, sense is heterogenous with the cipher of *lalangue*. I believe that, with the letter-symptom, Lacan was questioning, if not a possible end, then a limit to the ciphering by an element, the letter, that would not be heterogenous with the ciphering of phallic jouissance. Rather, the letter, by its fixity, identical to itself, would function as the One of the series of the decipherable ones, the One that constitutes them into a set, which makes of them something else than a powdery multiplicity. This is manifestly what he looks for when he says at the end of *Encore* that the signifier One, I quote, "It is the signifying order insofar as it is instituted on the basis of the envelopment by which the whole of the chain subsists" (Lacan, [1975] 1999, p. 143). We land here on the question of the One, of "There is something of the One" [*Y a de l'Un*]. A major formula, as much as "There is no relation" [*Y a pas du rapport*]. Lacan explores this question, he is even hell-bent on it, starting from "*D'un discours qui ne serait pas du semblant*". How is there something of the One with all the ones of differences constituted by the cipher-elements of *lalangue*. Where to find the unity-element of the series? The question posed at the end of *Encore* and posed again in the same way more than one year later in "La troisième". And what is the partner of the One, another one, or the Other?

This problem of the One Lacan tried to approach via logic, or rather logics, as there is more than one, the logic of sets being the most appropriate to matters of the unconscious, to the point where Lacan asks himself if it had been sparked by the Freudian discovery with which indeed it is contemporary. From these very sinuous developments, not always convergent but always complex, I came to extract a distinction which seems to me at the same time simple, consistent and operative. There are ones of "*moteriality*", made of linguistic matter, which are all, at the same time, Ones of jouissance; they all suppose the cipher which distinguishes the elements of *lalangue*. But they are diverse, these ones of "*moteriality*": the ones of the unconscious, a worker never on strike, they are the ones of repetition that cipher phallic jouissance, the jouissance that Lacan says "the One that makes a function of the subject" (Lacan, [2011] 2018, p. 219) and that we have the task to decipher in analysis. And then the One of the symptom, which differs by its fixity because it does not cease to write itself from the real. Is it this one that constitutes a limit, an end to the decipherable series, or only the sense? Sense, as I said, is heterogenous with the cipher. This is not the case with the letter which is of the One, distinct from the ones of the series because it is identical to itself, an exception, therefore, in relation to the series of the decipherable but whose jouissance is not reduced to phallic jouissance as said in "*La troisième*" (Lacan, 2011). It is opaque jouissance, Lacan will say, the true *extimate*. On the other hand, another type of One is the One of the saying *[dire]*, which is not "*moteriality*". It is existence; nothing else testifies to existence but the saying. It is a different real, the one of existential emergence and from which Lacan defines the one who speaks *[parlant]* finally as the One-saying of the One all alone that knows itself all alone, with the question of knowing which partner we can attribute to it, if not the symptom-partner. Therefore there is a coupling of the One-saying that knows itself to be all alone with the One of the symptom.

Lacan, in the seminar *The Sinthome*, makes of the *dit-mension* of the saying introduced in "L'étourdit" the origin of yet another One, the Borromean One, which is a triple-One or a One of the "chain-knot" *[chainoeud]*. Therefore, identifying with one's symptom becomes complex. Identification, no matter what it is, supposes the unary trait, UT, but which one? Is it only the One of the opaque jouissance of the letter, or also the One of sense, equally enjoyed but in a different way, not without the imaginary, or the Borromean One that knots them?

To identify oneself without identifying?

I am going back to my question: can one identify one's symptom?

When we started reading this symptom-letter in *RSI*, we saw a rush towards the supposed identification in the pass with the letter of the symptom, and this doxa, via the inevitable effect of the group, affected both *passants* and cartels. For me, who has listened to many testimonies over the years, it is certain that, in these efforts to identify one's own symptom-letter, one can apply what Lacan says about the deciphered unconscious at the end of *Encore*: it is a lucubration of knowledge upon *lalangue*, which remains hypothetical and can only produce a pseudo-assurance of the pass – which an assured pass does not need, but this can easily lead the collective astray. I am afraid that it corresponds less to the authenticity of the analysand's experience than to some objective of transmission in the dispositive *[dispositif]*, and, moreover, we see *passants* and passers, before engaging in their task, frantically studying everything that has been said about it previously.

I firstly point out that the notion of identification with the symptom does not concern what is at stake in the turning point *[virage]* of the pass but rather the result of a completed analysis. Furthermore, this so-called identification with the symptom-letter does not come from Lacan. I cannot find any remark from Lacan that pushes in that direction; in fact, it's quite the contrary. First of all, that the letter is defined as a unit of jouissance and identical to itself, a = a, does not say anything about the One by which it is defined. Is it rather the One that makes a set, a set of ones that remain uncertain, "from the phoneme to the whole of language" Lacan repeats – he even said that the letter does not make a set, it is the set – or, is it the One of the uncertain element, which is also made, from the phoneme to the phrase, of some "*moteriality*"? Let us at least leave the question pending because the only One that is certain is that of the saying [*dire*].

Let us neither forget that the truth condemned to be half-said never reaches either the real or unconscious knowledge. There where the unconscious was, the truth will never be. And Lacan concludes: "One starts to know in order not to attain it", ultimately. I do not forget what he also said about the slip of the tongue that, when it does not make any sense, we are in the unconscious, and "one knows it oneself" ["*on le sait soi*"]. But what this really means is that this knowledge cannot be transmitted; it is irremediably private and, above all, ephemeral since one exits it as soon as one gives it attention. In other words, one does not expose it except after having again passed to the lying truth outside the unconscious.

I am thus tempted to re-translate "identification with the symptom" into each one's identification with one's Borromean unarity [*unarité*], another One, as I have said, the one of the knotting between sense and real, between the opaque jouissance, which is parasitic, and that of sense – which is not. This knotting is being rectified all along by the saying of the analysis, by what is being written by the operation of speech. The knot presides over what I call, for lack of a better word, a metabolism of jouissances, neither wholly real, nor wholly mental, of which the subject can perceive the main constants. We see the benefit of the knotting: the leaking of sense, which falls under the inexorable blow of the half-said, is stopped by the real, which, however, is antinomic to any verisimilitude; but conversely, the autism of the opaque real is limited by sense, by the truth.

Therefore, to recognise the real outside sense is not to idealise it, and Lacan's indications go in the opposite direction to that idealisation. I recall what he said at the end of the second conference on Joyce about the jouissance proper to the letter-symptom as "jouissance, opaque by excluding sense". And well, analysis "devalorises" it through sense in order to "resolve" it, which supposes being the dupe . . . of the Father, he says, the Father being in that period the father-saying, the fourth consistency. And this is so true that the Father is the father-saying, about which he adds that Joyce succeeded in this devalorisation without passing through an analysis, through the saying of an analysis but by . . . his "art-saying" [*art-dire*]. Suffice it to say, if analysis is oriented towards the real, it is ultimately towards the real of the knot. It is what Lacan says when he speaks about the poem-unconscious, as a knotting of real and sense, the poem that I am, which was written without me and which I can sign, and signing is not the same as knowing. To sign the poem and to identify with the symptom are one and the same.

References

Freud, S. (1955 [1909]). Notes Upon a Case of Obsessional Neurosis. In: *The Standard Edition of the Complete Psychological Works of Sigmund Freud, Volume X (1909): Two Case Histories ('Little Hans' and the 'Rat Man')* (pp. 153–318). J. Strachey (Trans.). London: Hogarth Press.

Lacan, J. (1974). *Les non-dupes errent. Seminaire XXI (1973–1974) leçon du 9 avril 1974* [Unpublished manuscript].

Lacan, J. (1975). *R.S.I. Seminaire XXII (1974–1975) leçon du 21 Janvier 1975* [Unpublished manuscript].

Lacan, J. (1990 [1974]). *Television: A Challenge to the Psychoanalytic Establishment.* J. Copjec (Ed.). D. Hollier, R. Krauss, A. Michelson and J. Mehlman (Trans.). New York: Norton.

Lacan, J. (1999 [1975]). *The Seminar of Jacques Lacan, Book XX: Encore, On Feminine Sexuality, The Limits of Love and Knowledge 1972–1973.* B. Fink (Trans.). New York: Norton.

Lacan, J. (2001 [1973]). Introduction à l'édition allemande d'un premier volume des Écrits. In: *Autres écrits* (pp. 553–559). Paris: Éditions du Seuil.

Lacan, J. (2011). La Troisième. *La Cause freudienne*, no. 79, pp. 11–33.

Lacan, J. (2018 [2011]). *The Seminar of Jacques Lacan, Book XIX: . . . Or Worse 1971–1972.* A. R. Price (Trans.). Cambridge: Polity Press.

Index

For Product Safety Concerns and Information please contact our EU
representative GPSR@taylorandfrancis.com
Taylor & Francis Verlag GmbH, Kaufingerstraße 24, 80331 München, Germany

www.ingramcontent.com/pod-product-compliance
Lightning Source LLC
Chambersburg PA
CBHW070351270326
41926CB00017B/4086

9 780367 342036